NAC 201-1

# THE ARCANA OF SYMBOLISM

# THE ARCANA
# OF
# SYMBOLISM

by

W. B. CROW
D.Sc., Ph.D.

SAMUEL WEISER INC.
734 Broadway, New York N.Y. 10003

First Published October 1970

ISBN 0 87728 152 1

MADE AND PRINTED IN GREAT BRITAIN BY
THE GARDEN CITY PRESS LIMITED
LETCHWORTH, HERTFORDSHIRE
SG6 1JS

# CONTENTS

# Foreword

Although much may be said about symbolism from the philosophical point of view, the present volume is mainly concerned to show that, in the numerous details, there are traces of a common plan in the symbols of myth, legend, religion and the arcane lore of most diverse times and places. No treatment however is given of the myth which Sir James Frazer called the dying god (*The Golden Bough* : Part III, 1911), as this topic is to be dealt with fully in another work. Further, with reference to the Qabalah, we give a system of correspondences which is different from that used in the *Order of the Golden Dawn* and which has been used by many recent authors. We believe our Scheme is in harmony, both with earliest tradition, and with common sense.

Of course it may be argued that no system of correspondences which has been widely used and found to be satisfactory in practice, is wrong. As I repeatedly made clear in my *Mysteries of the Ancients* published some years ago (1941-1945) there is no absolute correspondence between Qabalah, Tarot and Astrology. Each system exists in its own right and is not quite the same as the others. If they were identical only one system would be needed. Nevertheless we have discovered how one of the planets (one only, not even one of the most favourable) has got himself promoted to a place among the supernals.

In mediaeval diagrams the planets were arranged in spheres around the earth. The most rapidly moving were often placed nearest, although these diagrams vary. Consequently the order was, as correctly placed from the earth outwards : Luna (the moon), Mercury, Venus, Sol (the sun), Mars, Jupiter, Saturn, the Zodiac, the Primum Mobile and the Empyreum. Now the last named was called 'a mystery which no man can comprehend'. It was regarded as the special resort of the deity and therefore was left out of charts designed only for the observation of the heavens. These charts also put the earth in the lowest place. Because such charts were not so concerned with the mysteries of religion as with astronomical observation, the arrangement gave the first three, working from the top downwards, as (i) Primum Mobile, (ii) Zodiac and (iii) Saturn. This is apparently incorrect.

In our view, a desirable arrangement for the study of the Mysteries is as follows :

**Kether** = Sphere of the Empyreum.

**Chokmah** = Sphere of the Primum Mobile.

**Binah** = Sphere of the Zodiac.

**Geburah** = Sphere of Saturn.

**Chesed** = Sphere of Jupiter.

**Netzach** = Sphere of Mars.

**Tiphareth** = Sphere of the Sun.

**Hod** = Sphere of Venus.

**Yesod** = Sphere of Mercury.

**Malkuth** = Sphere of the Moon.

We are not claiming this is the only possible view, however, but we are advising those who have not yet used it to try it out.

*Note.* Except where otherwise mentioned, the Biblical references are taken from the Douai-Rheims version, 1914.

# THE ARCANA OF SYMBOLISM

# CHAPTER I

# The Nature of Symbols

## Symbols and Signs

A symbol is a sign, but not all signs are symbols. A sign
is something connected with something else which, when it
appears, indicates this other thing. A traffic light is a sign, but
it is not a symbol. It has been consciously selected in a purely
arbitrary fashion to indicate something. A symbol, on the
other hand, has naturally appeared and has been carried on
by tradition. No one ever invented a symbol, it just grew up.
It survived by tradition. Those who view tradition with dis-
favour eschew symbolism.

## Language

Language is a system of spoken and written signs which
are largely symbolic. Many languages of a group have a large
number of common roots, all of which are symbols. On the
other hand modern technology has resulted in the invention
of a vast number of new words, many of which are entirely
arbitrary and have little connection with ancient roots,
although it must be admitted that some distinguished scientists have a genius for coining from ancient roots some words
which have just the right connotation for new phenomena.
Nevertheless such artificial language tends to consist of signs
which are not symbols.

Some recent writers have made the distinction between
words and the things they signify the source of many insoluble
problems. It is only too obvious, of course, as Goethe long
ago pointed out, that words are often used in place of real

explanations, but merely verbal expressions can easily be unmasked, precisely by talking about them.

In the Middle Ages St. Albertus Magnus pointed out that many words then in use were assigned a meaning other than that implied by their derivation. But few authors were more aware of the power of words, even if he did not write the magical treatises which are often regarded as his works.

## Depth Psychology

The present century has witnessed the development of the psychology of the unconscious as it is called, or depth psychology. The last term refers to the fact that some psychiatrists believe they have found hitherto undiscovered depths of the mind, wherein have been disclosed certain forms or patterns, controlling the behaviour of the individual. These were at first regarded as somewhat pathological, although admittedly occurring in most individuals, and were called *complexes*. Later, at least in the Zürich school (the followers of C. G. Jung) attention was drawn to certain inherited dispositions, called *archetypes*, retained in the collective unconscious. All these schools of thought recognize symbolism in the unconscious.

## Kinds of Symbols

Almost everything in nature and culture can act as a symbol, as Goethe taught. Stars and planets, metals and crystals, plants and animals, shapes and movements of the human body, are all symbolic. Their symbolism needs much study. The easiest symbols to understand are numbers, words and gestures. The gestures show clearly the difference between symbol and arbitrary sign. Such natural movements as nodding, laughing, grimacing, beckoning and hand-shaking are immediately understood in their social context, whereas the deaf-and-dumb hand language is largely made up of artificial signs.

Although symbols, as distinct from arbitrary signs, arise in the unconscious, that does not mean they are immediately understandable. Like language, other symbols have to be learned. Once learned, however, the symbol, if correctly given, can be seen to be correct, just as a child sees its multiplication tables (which he has had to learn) to be correct if he is sufficiently industrious to test them out.

Symbols, including numbers and languages, are gradually evolved during the history of mankind. It is true one speaks of the discovery of the zero, of fractions and of different kinds of calculus. But here the word discovery is used in the true sense of uncovering something which actually exists and it would be wrong to speak of the invention of these things. One could speak of the invention of a bicycle, an engine or an aeroplane, since these are purely conscious productions. But of course there are different grades or stages between discovery and invention, just as there are stages between the unconscious and the conscious.

## Myth

Mythology is the richest source of symbols. Myth is the language of religion. All the ancient religions were mystery religions and manifested through symbols. All the sacred books of the world, including the Bible, are written in symbolic language. None of the ancients, with few exceptions, doubted the power of symbols, although there were numerous disputes about the nature of the symbolic entities.[1]

Not until relatively late classical times do we read of materialistic objections to mythology. Lucretius (*circa* 96–55 B.C.) was the best known Roman writer who attacked religion in his poem *De Rerum Natura*. He is said to have committed

---

[1] Thus the *asuras* or god-like beings of the *Rig-Veda* were later regarded as satanic powers by the Zoroastrians.

suicide. However, soon after, the Christian religion became dominant in Europe and in spite of persecutions held its own for many centuries.[2] The first doubts began to spread with the so-called Reformation. At first these concerned only certain points of religion. But the very lowest depth was reached when Galileo (1564–1642) declared that the Universe consisted of nothing but matter of various shapes and sizes, moving in space and time. He said that tastes, smells, colours and feelings were nothing but names. Later John Locke (1632–1704) made the curious distinction between primary and secondary qualities. Only the former, he maintained, were real. The secondary qualities which included colours, sounds, tastes and smells were, as Locke says (I quote) 'nothing in the objects themselves'. This absurdity was followed by many, including Newton (1642–1727) and was copied, as I have pointed out elsewhere[3] 'by innumerable lesser scientists and writers, ignoring all the great philosophers of classical times and the Middle Ages'.

## Physical and Psychical Facts

As can be seen from the beginning of any text-book of physics, the students of this science reduce all phenomena to matter, energy, space and time. Materialists are naïve enough to imagine that these are the only categories of things that exist. They tell us an object is real if you can see and touch it. They would have us believe that real objects have no colour, no smell and no taste! They say, for instance, that colours are *only* vibrations of different wave-lengths, which can be determined by experiment. We do not for a moment deny that each colour can correspond with a different wave-length. But it turns out, by these same experiments, that the wave-length

[2] It is only very recently that religion has been opposed, on a large scale, in the East, under the influence of communism.
[3] W. B. Crow : The Exploration of the Psyche : *Astrological Magazine*, India, Jan. 1964.

of violet is further removed from that of red than it is from that of green, when it is obvious to all who are not colour-blind, that red resembles violet much more than green. So it is clear that the wave-length theory is only part of the truth, and a very misleading part.

Colours, feelings and thoughts are perfectly real. The propositions of mathematics, which are purely mental, are obvious to any mind that grasps them. It is impossible to deny them. It is just as useless to argue about the truths of aesthetics, ethics, myth and religion.

## Qabalah

Many years ago, in an article in the Journal *Psyche*[4] the present writer suggested that the comparative study of myths should be conducted along the same lines as comparative anatomy. Just in the same way as we compare, for instance, the skeleton of the horse, bone for bone, with the skeleton of man, so we might compare each god of the Japanese pantheon with, say, that of the classical Greeks. But it is only when we come to study the details of the Holy Qabalah, and the original Tarot, that we find, so to speak, the skeleton of mythology, that is, the basic pattern to which all the myths of the world conform.

The Qabalah belongs to the Hebrew tradition. The sacred lore of the Jews fell into three sections : (*i*) the Old Testament which they called *the Law*, the first five books (the Pentateuch) being the most important; (*ii*) the Talmud, which was a commentary on the preceding, studied by learned rabbis, and which was called *the Soul of the Law*, and (*iii*) the Qabalah which was at first secret knowledge, not written down, and imparted to high initiates only. It was called *the Soul of the Soul of the Law*. It has only partly been revealed in writing, and that only in relatively recent times.

Probably the two best qabalistic books are the *Sepher*

[4] The inherited factors in human behaviour, *Psyche,* 1929.

*Yetzirah* or book of formation[5] and the *Sepher ha Zohar* or book of splendour. The first is the earliest and shortest. It was written in Hebrew and its author is supposed to be Akiba or Akibha ben Joseph, a rabbi of the first century A.D. It first appeared in print as a Latin translation by William Postel published in Paris in 1552. Ten years later the original Hebrew was printed at Mantua. Many editions in various languages were later available. The *Zohar* is ascribed to Rabbi Moses ben Leon, 1290, in Spain, and was first printed in Hebrew in 1558, at Mantua. Translations were afterwards made. Most of what is related subsequently in this connection derives from the *Sepher Yetzirah*, but the *Zohar*, which is enormously long, contains also a system of ceremonial magic, from which, according to F. de P. Castells,[6] the ritual of the Holy Royal Arch degree is derived and much of the craft degrees, so the author thinks the origin of freemasonry was from the Qabalah.

**The Tarot**

The Tarot is a pack of playing cards. All the early playing cards in Europe are tarots. They appeared in the thirteenth or fourteenth century. Where they came from is not now known. But they were associated with the gypsies, as the latter were wandering about Europe in considerable numbers, and no doubt helped to spread the cards and use them for the damnable practice of fortune telling, as they use the modern cards today. The latter are derived from the tarot pack by leaving out many of the cards. To be precise, the Tarot included seventy-eight cards, whilst the modern pack only has fifty-three, counting the Joker, which is not used in many games.

The Tarot is evidently the work of initiates. Among theosophical circles we frequently hear of masters of wisdom, hidden in remote places in Asia, such as the Himalayas. They believe

[5] *Sepher* means book in Hebrew.
[6] *Origin of the Masonic Degrees,* London, not dated.

themsclves to be somehow responsible for the welfare of mankind. They form a group or lodge which has existed from remote ages.

Now the story goes that, in the early days of the so-called Reformation, the Masters or Initiates of this group began to panic, for they were much afraid that the secret knowledge of symbols might die out in the world. So they met together to devise some method of preserving it. All sorts of schemes were suggested, but at last the ingenious idea was adopted of putting the symbols of the ancient wisdom into a set of cards for playing games. It was thought that at least the symbols would be then preserved. The initiates actually made one mistake. There were too many cards. Players simplified the pack. They threw away all the twenty-two most important symbols except one, which has remained as the Joker. Do not ask whether this story is true, but it is as good an explanation as any. After all, the Tarot is not lost. It was preserved as a curiosity in museums, where we find it today. It has even been reprinted for foolish people to tell fortunes. It also serves, as it happens, for study, as the Masters intended. So perhaps they were not so mistaken after all!

## The Classification of Symbols

The great interest of the Qabalah is that it corresponds with almost all, if not all, other systems of symbolism. It has a very exact relation to the Tarot, as we shall see.

Any modern book on the Qabalah will give a diagram of the Tree of Life. On the latter, a human figure called Adam Kadmon is sometimes shown suspended or enthroned. The tree is said to show how God manifests in the Universe. It explains creation, incarnation and all forms of manifestations. Everything, it is said, can be classified by its means.

The Tree has on it ten *sephiroth* (singular *sephira*) symbolized by pomegranates. These are spiritual entities, manifesting as steps in creation. Only a very simplified account can be given here, since we cannot follow up all the intricacies of qabalistic thought in the space at our disposal. However it must be said that, in addition to the ten sephiroth there are twenty-two paths of wisdom connecting them. Of these paths, ten correspond with the ten sephiroth. The reason for this correspondence is to show, amongst other things, that the sephiroth, although in themselves of enormous importance, cannot exist entirely independently, but are all linked together.

The idea of the four worlds played a part in developed qabalism. We need only mention one aspect. The Tree of Life was sometimes divided into four, as follows: (*i*) the world of archetypes (*Atziluth*) which comprised the first Sephira; (*ii*) the world of Creation (*Briah*) which comprises the second and third sephira; (*iii*) the world of formation (*Yetzirah*) includes the fourth, fifth, sixth, seventh, eighth and ninth sephira and (*iv*) the world of activity or material world (*Assiah*) has in it only the tenth or last sephira.

If we now examine the sephiroth we find they are arranged in three pillars, best called pillars of justice and mercy at the sides, with the pillar of harmony between them, in the middle.

Kether or the crown, also called Abbah or Father, is the first sephira. It is at the top of the middle pillar.

Chokmah or Wisdom, sometimes called the Son or Logos is at the top of the pillar of mercy.

Binah or understanding intelligence or spirit, sometimes called Immah, the Mother or Queen, is at the top of the pillar of Justice.

The first three are called the three supernals and represent the supreme triad or Trinity. The last seven represent the planets of astrology.[7]

Geburah, called strength or Justice, is second down on the

---

[7] We follow the diagram given in Kircher: *Oedipus Aegypticus,* Rome, 1652, which appears to represent the correct traditional attributions. Other arrangements have been tried, but we have not found them satisfactory, see Foreword.

pillar of that name. That it corresponds with Saturn is indicated by the fact that it is also called Pechad or fear, also severity, both referring to the sinister nature of that planet.

Chesed, called magnificence or mercy, is second down on the pillar of that name. Its astrological correspondence agrees precisely with the planet Jupiter.

Tiphereth, called grace, majesty or sovereignty, is second down in the middle pillar and obviously belongs to the sun.

Third down and lowermost on the pillar of mercy is Netzach or Nizah, called victory, obviously corresponding with the planet Mars.

Its opposite number, third down and lowermost on the pillar of justice is Hod, called glory, honour or splendour, corresponding with the planet Venus.

Yesod, third down on the middle pillar and called foundation, corresponds with the planet Mercury.

Malkuth, an additional sephira, fourth down on the middle pillar, is called Kingdom or bride, and is assigned to the moon.

As previously referred to, there are ten paths corresponding with these ten sephiroth. There remain twelve paths which must be assigned to the twelve signs of the Zodiac.

## Hebrew Letters

The qabalists also say that the twenty-two letters of the Hebrew alphabet correspond with the twenty-two paths of the Holy Qabalah. Moreover they say that there are three *mother letters*, Aleph, Mem and Shin, which represent the three supernals. Then there are seven double letters, which correspond with the seven planets. These double letters are so called because, when they have a special mark on them, called a daish, they are pronounced differently. Finally the remaining twelve, called single letters, are assigned to the twelve signs of the zodiac. Therefore the twenty-two letters of the Hebrew alphabet correspond with the twenty-two paths, thus :

3 = the triad or Trinity, the three supernals or mother-letters;

7 = the seven planets or double letters;

12 = the Zodiac, composed of twelve signs or single letters.

One must not forget that the qabalist have:

4 = the four divisions of the Tree of Life.

## The Tarot Analysed

Let us now examine the Tarot. As already stated, this comprises seventy-eight cards. There are four suits of fourteen cards each, making fifty-six cards. They are called *trumps minor*. The four suits are (*i*) cups or chalices, (*ii*) discs, coins or plates, (*iii*) wands, batons, rods or staves and (*iv*) swords. Each suit contains ten pip cards and four honours. The latter, in ascending order of value, are knave or servant, knight, queen and king. But in all there are only fifty-six, which leaves twenty-two to be accounted for. These additional twenty-two cards are all pictures and are called *atouts* or *trumps major*. Each card is numbered, but there are only twenty-one numbers in the ordinary sense, since one of the cards counts as zero.

As some of our readers may not be familiar with them, we append a list of the trumps major: **0** *The Fool*, **1** *The Conjuror* or *Magician*, **2** *The High Priestess* or *Pope Joan*, **3** *The Empress*, **4** *The Emperor*, **5** *The High Priest* or *Pope*, **6** *The Lovers, with Cupid*, **7** *The Chariot*, **8** *Justice* (female figure bearing sword and balance), **9** *The Hermit*, **10** *The Wheel of Fortune* (with two figures, often monkeys, one ascending, the other descending), **11** *Fortitude* or *Strength* (a female figure, forcing open a lion's mouth), **12** *The Hanged Man* (a male figure suspended upside down from a horizontal bar by one leg, the other crossed), **13** *Death* (a skeleton with a scythe), **14** *Temperance* (a female figure pouring liquid from one vessel to another), **15** *The Devil* (a winged figure, often with victims), **16** *The Blasted*

*Tower* (a tall building struck by lightning, usually with a pair of figures falling from it), **17** *The Star* (one large star, sometimes seven smaller stars and below a female figure pouring water), **18** *The Moon* (with two dogs and a crayfish below), **19** *The Sun* (with a child on a white horse below), **20** *The Last Judgement* (an angel blowing a trumpet above, the dead emerging from their tombs below), **21** *The World* or *Universe* (a dancing figure, male or often female, surrounded by a wreath with the symbols of the four evangelists in the corners, ox, lion, eagle and man).

Elsewhere[8] we have pointed out how the trumps major may correspond with (*i*) the three supernals, (*ii*) the seven planets and (*iii*) with the twelve signs of the zodiac. The suits or trumps minor correspond with the four worlds or four elements. These correspondences are to be dealt with in the following chapters.

[8] W. B. Crow : The Symbolism of Chess and Cards, *Mysteries of the Ancients* No. 13, London, 1944.

# CHAPTER II

# The Supernals

## The Old Testament

Although the unity of God is most strongly emphasized in the Old Testament, there are passages wherein God speaks of Himself in the plural. Thus in *Gen* i, 26 God said: 'Let Us make man in our image . . . In *Gen* iii, 22, speaking of Adam, God says he 'is become as one of Us' . . . In *Gen* xi, 7 on seeing the tower of Babel, God said: 'Let Us go down' . . . with the idea of confounding the builders. Finally, in *Is* vi, 8 the Lord speaks of Himself both in the singular and the plural, saying: 'Whom shall I send and who shall go for Us?' The first three of these undoubtedly refer to the Supernals and the Church Fathers said they refer to the Christian Trinity. The fourth item may refer, however, in the plural, to the Seraphim (the highest angels) who have previously been mentioned in that chapter.

Modern critics have claimed that the plural form (We) was only a mark of dignity as it was used by Persian and Greek kings, and afterward by sovereigns in Europe, as it still is in official documents. But the Bible probably precedes such usage and in any case such rulers first used it because it was believed that they were God's representatives on earth. There is little doubt that three was a sacred number among the Jews and the three Supernals represented different ways of representing the Godhead, each really distinct but each wholly divine.

In *Gen* xviii the Lord appears unto Abraham in the form of three men and Abraham hastens to his wife Sara and asks her to prepare three measures of flour. Elsewhere they are spoken of as the One Lord. In the early Christian Church the three were taken to be symbols of the Holy Trinity. There is also reference to the Logos or Word of God, *e.g. Gen* xv, 4 and the spirit of God, *e.g. Gen* i, 2.

The number three is often used in the Old Testament to signify completeness. In *Ez* xiv, 14 three men passed through the three phases of creation, destruction and restoration : Noe (Noah) of the whole world, Daniel of the Jewish world of Jerusalem and Job of his own personal world. Three men were cast into the fiery furnace and survived (*Dan* iii, 22–95). The three sons of Noe peopled the world after the flood (*Gen* x). There were three cities of refuge on the East of the river Jordan, and three on the West (*Numbers* xxxv). Job had three friends (*Job* ii, 11). Joshua sent out three men to explore the land of Canaan (*Jos* xviii, 4). Isaias (Isaiah) was a hermit, naked and barefoot, for three years, as a sign, (*Is* xx, 3). Samuel was called three times (*I Kings—I Samuel* King James version iii, 4–8). Elias stretched and measured himself thrice against the widow's son to revive him (*III Kings=I Kings* King James version 21, 22). Jonas (Jonah) (*Jon* ii, 1) was in the great fish three days and nights. Quite a number of other examples will occur to students of the Old Testament, especially in prophetic passages.

## The New Testament

In the Epistles of St. John (*I John* v, 7) there is a reference to the dogma of the Christian Trinity. It was put in to support the logos doctrine which is, as is well known, fully expounded in the Gospel of St. John. It says there are three that give testimony in heaven, the Father, the Word or Son, and the Holy Ghost or Spirit and these three are One.

In A.D. 325 the dogma of the complete Divinity of Christ was upheld at the first Oecumenical Council at Nicaea against the sect of the Arians, who long troubled the Church. In

A.D. 381 at the Second Oecumenical Council at Constantinople the complete Divinity of the Holy Ghost was upheld against the Macedonians. The dogma of the Holy Trinity has seldom been questioned, even among Protestants.

The number three is a most important symbol in the New Testament. Soon after His birth Jesus was visited by three wise men or Magi, from the East, who offered Him three gifts : gold, frankincense and myrrh (*Matt* ii, 11). At the baptism of Jesus the Holy Trinity were represented, by Jesus Himself, by the Father in a voice from Heaven, and the Holy Ghost descending in the form of a dove (*Matt* iii, 16, 17; *Mark* i, 9–11; *Luke* iii, 21, 22). At the Transfiguration Jesus took three apostles (Peter, James and John) as witnesses and a threefold vision appeared (Jesus with Moses and Elias). Peter suggests they shall build three tabernacles (*Matt* xvii, 1–8, *Mark* ix, 1–8, *Luke* ix, 28–36). In *I Corinthians* xviii, 13 the three great virtues are named : faith, hope and charity. The drama of the death, entombment and resurrection of Christ is spread over three days. Jesus prayed thrice in the garden of Gethsemane (*Matt* xxvi, 39–44). He said the temple should be destroyed and rebuilt again in three days, referring to the resurrection (*Matt* xxvi, 61). He said to Peter thrice 'Lovest thou me?' (*John* xxi, 15–17). He also foresaw the threefold denial (*Matt* xxvi, 34). The Holy Family consisted of three : Jesus, Mary and Joseph. St. Patrick used the leaf of shamrock, with its three leaves, to symbolize the Holy Trinity. In Christian ritual the number three often occurs as instanced in the three effusions at Baptism.

## The Koran

The Muhammadan or Moslem Religion (Islam) rejects the doctrine of the Trinity. The *Koran* says that God cannot be the third of three (*Surah* iv, 169). Moslems deny that Jesus died on the cross and think someone else in His likeness took his place thereon (*Surah* iv, 155, 156).

Nevertheless, Moslem theology has three symbols connected with God. The first thing created by God or that co-existed with Him, it was said, was *qalam,* the pen which recorded all the things to be created. Next came the tablet or scroll called *lauh* which recorded all the decrees of God. Finally there was the *'arsh* or throne of God. The tablet or scroll has been identified by some authors as the *Koran* itself, which they say has existed from all eternity. Others identify it with the *logos.* To the philosophers the Pen represented the Prime Intellect or First Reason, the tablet or scroll the Second Reason and the throne the Third Reason.

Some Moslem theologians refer to three divine entities : (*i*) God, (*ii*) the light of God and (*iii*) the light of the Prophet. In the *Koran (Surah* XLVII) the signs given to infidels are mentioned. They were said to be three (*i*) the mission of Muhammad (*ii*) the splitting of the moon and (*iii*) the day of darkness when smoke descended from heaven. The Sufis who are Islamic mystics say there are three aids to devotion (*i*) attraction (*ii*) the path and (*iii*) ascent to divine things.

## Classical Mythology

Turning now to the beliefs of pre-Christian Greece and Rome we enter an entirely different world. Their numerous gods were admitted by the educated classes to be symbolic, with the proviso that the symbol was usually taken to be something infinitely more serious than is popularly believed at the present day. The great philosophers, such as Plato (427–347 B.C.) and Aristotle (384–322 B.C.) often used mythological language.

The Romans took over the Greek pantheon, with some additions from the Etruscans. This group of gods, although containing elements derived from the Egyptian, Cretan and Phoenician, is very different from any of the latter. In fact its origin is largely unknown. Rather full details of the gods and their adventures are given in the works of Homer (before

850 B.C.) and Hesiod (eighth century B.C.) among the Greeks and Ovid (43 B.C.–A.D. 17) among the Romans, but very many authors must be consulted over a long period.[1]

The first triad or group of three appears to be generally recognized as Chaos, Coelus or Uranus (heaven) and Gaea or Tellus (earth). Chaos, in Hesiod, is scarcely recognized as a god, but represents the original void. Much later Chaos was identified with the Roman Janus and given an historical character. Uranus sometimes appears as the son of Chaos and Gaea, the last named as the wife of Chaos.

Uranus mated with his mother Gaea and she gave birth to (i) the twelve titans, (ii) the three Cyclopes and (iii) the three Hecatoncheires. These are *three* different groups and the last two consist of *three* each. The cyclopes were one-eyed monsters and gave rise to a whole race of such beings, one of which figures in an incident in the *Odyssey*. The hecatoncheires are described as enormous hundred-handed, fifty-headed giants.

Of the Titans the leader was the youngest, called Cronus or Saturn. The Titans rebelled against Uranus and Saturn took his place, having castrated his father. The eldest of the Titans allowed Saturn to become world-ruler provided he promised to produce no heirs. So Saturn 'swallowed', *i.e.* imprisoned his own children when they were born but the youngest, Zeus or Jupiter, escaped. Later Jupiter dethroned Saturn and set up *three* kingdoms. Jupiter himself became the ruler of heaven, his brother Poseidon or Neptune of the realm of the sea and his other brother Pluto of the underworld. Thus the triad play a very important part in the mythology of Greece and Rome.

In the *Eleusinian Mysteries* the god Dionysus (Bacchus) and the goddess Demeter (Ceres) played the main parts. Dionysus was the son of Zeus (Jupiter) and Demeter one of

---

[1] The reader might find it advantageous to consult a classical dictionary whilst reading this section, if not familiar with the classics.

the seven wives of Zeus.[2] Dionysus was God of Wine and Demeter the Goddess of Wheat or Corn. It may be thought that Zeus, Dionysus and Demeter foreshadow the Christian Trinity. Demeter is sometimes called a virgin goddess, sometimes mother of Dionysus. These mysteries have also been compared with the Christian Mass or Eucharist, wine and bread being miraculously transformed therein.

Besides this the number three constantly recurs in Classical Mythology. Jupiter's thunderbolt[3] was three-forked. Neptune's trident[4] was three-pronged. Pluto's dog had three heads, Pluto as king of the underworld only had a sceptre with two prongs, but his realm had three times three rivers and the most important one flowed round thrice three times. Moreover there were three judges of the underworld and three Furies were sent out therefrom. Further, there were supposed to be three Fates who ruled the lives of all: Clotho with a distaff presides over birth, Lachesis with a spinning wheel is thought to spin out destiny and Atropos, with scissors, as cutting the thread of life was supposed to rule over death. Among monsters we must not forget the three Gorgons, winged females, with snakes for hair and tusks like those of a wild boar. They turned people to stone with their looks. Then there were the Graiae, grey-haired women with only one eye and one tooth between them, which were passed round. We have already mentioned the Cyclops and the Hecatoncheires, even more frightful. There were three Horae, daughters of Jupiter and Themis: Eunomia, Dike and Eirene, who presided over the year and three Charities or Graces, daughters of Jupiter and Venus, beautiful maidens, in constant attendance on their mother. Perhaps we ought to mention the three times three Muses, who symbolized the arts and sciences, and attended Apollo.

[2] In another myth Dionysus was the son of a mortal woman.

[3] The thunderbolt is a ritual object. It has been retained in Tibetan Lamaism. It has symmetrical forked ends.

[4] A better known myth; also retained in Lamaism. It is only forked at one end.

The Roman idea that there were three chief gods was possibly carried on from the Etruscan as well as from the Greek. Of the Cretan pantheon we only know for certain that there was a precursor of Zeus and a semblance of a young man or child and his mother called 'The Lady'. Of the Phoenician a rather sinister triad of the gods, Mot (death) and Kolpia (logos) and the goddess Baaut (darkness) have been cited, but relatively little is known about them.

### Egyptian Mythology

During the long period during which the ancient Egyptian religion held sway, from prehistoric times to the Moslem invasion in A.D. 638 the main features of the mythology remained unchanged. There were, of course, some breaks, for instance when the heretic Akhnaton (Amenophis IV) who reigned[5] 1372–54 B.C. tried, successfully for a few years, to abolish the worship of the gods and substitute the sole worship of the sun's disc. But on his death the full pantheon was soon restored. Even as late as the Roman occupation the cult continued, the Roman Emperor being recognized as Pharaoh and adopting Egyptian customs.

The land of Egypt consisted, under the Pharaohs, of Upper and Lower Egypt, and was further subdivided into divisions called *nomes*. In each nome a triad, representing the supreme godhead, was worshipped, but generally in different nomes, and to some extent at different times in the history, different names were used for the members of the triad. However the best known was the group Osiris, his wife Isis and his son Horus. The cult of Osiris lasted over about two thousand years.[6] It took over from many other groups. The figures of Isis and the babe Horus closely resemble the later (Christian) figures of Madonna and Child. Moreover, one of the three

---

[5] Illegally according to his successors; see Posener *et al.* : *Dict. Egyptian Civilization,* London, trans., 1962.

[6] Posener *et al., loc. cit.*

was sacrificed, being killed and resurrected only in this instance, it seems, it was the Father and not the Son, as in the Christian religion. Nevertheless the Egyptians, after death, hoped to become at one with Osiris, just as Christians hope to be united with Christ.

## Babylonian Mythology

As in the Graeco-Roman mythology the Babylonian genealogy of the gods commences with shadowy figures. There is a primitive triad : Apsu the sweet waters, Tiamat the bitter waters and their son Mommu. At first all three were feminine and two later (Apsu and Mommu) apparently changed their sex. However, all these were eventually deposed or destroyed and a more permanent triad of Anu, Enlil and Ea were worshipped. Anu was the sky-god, Enlil the earth-god and Ea, the water-god who was identified with Oannes, half-man and half-fish, a great culture hero. Enlil, a rather sinister character, was later transformed into, or replaced by, the relatively benign Marduk, known as Bel (Lord)[7] and thought to have been mentioned in the Old Testament.

The Hittites were a mysterious people, mentioned in the Old Testament, who occupied much of Asia Minor *circa* 2000 B.C. to 1190 B.C. Their mythology, however, seems to be very similar to that of the Babylonians, for they had a sacred triad of chief gods, whose names have been given as Anu, Alalu and Ea.

## Zoroastrian Mythology

The Zoroastrian religion is named after a religious teacher called Zoroaster or Zarasthustra who probably lived in the sixth century B.C. He was either the founder, or the reformer, of the religion of Persia, which was the state religion until replaced by the Shiite Muhammadan cult in A.D. 661. A few

[7] The title Bel was, of course, applied to several gods.

Zoroastrians still exist, mostly in the Bombay region of India. This religion was alleged to be dualistic and the conflict with the evil principle (Ahriman) is certainly emphasized. But there are or were originally three good principles, holding the supreme place: Zervan Akarana, Mithra and Ahura Mazda or Ormuzd.

The name Mithra is connected with Mitra, a god of the Vedic religion of early India. Whilst his cult died out in India it became popular in Persia and in Roman times spread into Europe, as is attested by numerous archaeological remains. Mithra represented the sun. His religion was a rival to Christianity, but had a complex initiatory system which excluded women. In the second century it spread rapidly in the Roman army and even reached Britain, as shown by the remains of temples. The figure of Mithras was represented in a cave. He holds in one hand a bull by one of its horns and with the other hand is plunging a dagger into the animal's neck. Below, a serpent and other creatures are licking up the blood. This is believed to be a rival sacrificial cult to that of the Christian Lamb of God.

### Hindu Mythology

The religion of the Hindus may be divided into two main periods: the Vedic and the Brahminic. The early gods of the Vedas were, however, taken over by the latter, and although some of them were reduced in rank to minor deities the two systems were inextricably merged. However, in both periods there were three great gods, now known as Brahma, Vishnu and Shiva.

Brahma is universally admitted to be the first person of this holy triad. He is eternal, of course, but springs periodically into manifestation from the egg deposited by Himself as first cause. He is thus Hiranagarbha in the Vedas.

Vishnu is the second person. He is eternal and divine but nevertheless becomes human as an *avatar* or incarnation,

Krishna. He also has ten partial avatars, one of which (Bala-rama) is an elder brother of Krishna, reminding one of John the Baptist, forerunner and cousin of Jesus. Vishnu is of little importance in the Vedic period.

Shiva is the third person and has many of the qualities of the third supernal of the Qabalah. He is known as Rudra in the Vedas.

There is considerable resemblance of this triad to the Christian Trinity. The three persons are really One God. The second person is true God and true man, as Krishna. Whilst temples are frequently dedicated to Vishnu and Shiva, we are told[8] there is only one in India dedicated to the first person. It is therefore of interest that in Europe, whilst many churches are dedicated to Christ (*e.g.* as St. Saviour, etc.) and to the Holy Ghost (*e.g.* as Church of the Holy Spirit), we have yet to dis-cover one named specifically after the Father or first Person.

The Hindu had several references to the number three in their mythological philosophy. In the latter, the three *gunas* played an important part. The gunas were modes of cosmic manifestation. They were (*i*) *Tamas* which was inertia or inactivity, symbolized by a descending line; (*ii*) *Sattva* was rhythm or harmony, symbolized by a horizontal line and (*iii*) Rajas was activity, symbolized by an ascending line.

The three lettered word AUM, used as a symbol of Brah-man, the one god, is probably equivalent to the Hebrew mother letters in spite of differences. The three prongs of the trident of Shiva and his three eyes have much the same sig-nificance.

### Norse Mythology

In the second edition of Egerton Syke's *Dictionary of Non-Classical Mythology*[9] the supplement mentions a passage in

[8] J. S. M. Ward : *Freemasonry and the Ancient Gods,* London, 1921.
   [9] London, 1961.

the second chapter of the *Prose Edda* referring to the Trinity of Nordic myth, the names being (*i*) Thridi, the high, (*ii*) Janfar, the equally high and (*iii*) and Har, the third. The last named suggests Hara, which in the body of the work is given as a Vedic name for Rudra or Shiva.

But by far the best known names for the Teutonic triad are Odin, Wili and We. They appear at the beginning of a new universe and play a part in creation. Wili (or Vili) may have been identical with Lodehur, and We or Ve with Hoenir. Odin is, of course, the best known of the three. He appears as a man and even as a sacrifice. The other two are little known except as creators. Odin, Hoenir and Lodehur gave life to the first three human beings. According to F. Kauffmann[10] however, Lodehur is the same as Thor and Hoenir as Tyr.

The Norsemen imagined that there were three *Norns* which closely correspond with the three Fates of the Classics. They were named Urda, the past; Verdandi, the present and Skulda, the future.

### Keltic Mythology

The Keltic peoples in the first century B.C. occupied France (called Gaul by the Romans), Spain and Portugal (called Iberia) and the British Isles. They were gradually being forced back by the Romans. In Gaul there were three supreme gods called Teutates, Hesus or Esus and Tharamis or Taranis,[11] which are probably names given to them by the Romans when fighting in Gaul. This perhaps accounts for them all being described as war-gods. Later the Romans identified them with their own gods, probably to appease the people. Tharamis became Jupiter, as both wielded the thunder, Hesus was supposed to be Mars and Teutates, who presided over letters, Mercury. The name Hesus suggests Jesus but there is little evidence for any connection. Hesus has been

[10] *Northern Mythology,* London, 1903.
[11] Lucan : *Pharsalia,* first century A.D.

identified with the Welsh god Hu, also with the Egyptian Osiris. Their symbol was a bull.

The Druids were the priests, law-givers and initiated teachers of the Keltic peoples, as will be known to most readers. Much of their lore made use of the number three, hence the celebrated Druidic triads. They believed in three forms of God, symbolized by the letters OIV. There were three worlds (*i*) Ceugant, the world of God; (*ii*) Gwynvyd, the world of animate and immortal beings and (*iii*) Abred, the world of matter. There were three obligations of man.[12] These triads survived into Arthurian literature: there were three closures and three fatal disclosures, three holy tribes of Britain and three disloyal ones, three blessed rulers and three diademed chiefs, three chief ladies of Britain, three beautiful women, three counselling knights, three great astronomers, three learned knights and three golden-tongued knights, three battle knights and three stayers of slaughter, three ardent lovers, three makers of golden shoes and three tribe herdsmen.[13]

The three closures and disclosures are extremely curious and call for some explanation. The head of the great king and culture-hero Bran or Vran was cut off as a relic when he died and for a time acted as an oracle. Eventually it was buried under the White Tower of London. While it remained it was supposed, by its magic, to prevent the invasion of Britain. This was the first closure. But later King Arthur had it dug up, in that he preferred to hold Britain by force of arms. This was the first fatal disclosure or unfortunate uncovering. The second closure was the burial of the bones of Vortimer, buried near the chief harbour, believed to prevent, by their magical power, any approach of a hostile vessel or fleet. The bones were dug up by Vortigern and this was the second fatal disclosure. The third closure was the burial of

[12] Lewis Spence: *The Mysteries of Britain*, Aquarian Press, 1970 Edition.
[13] All these are included in E. Cobham Brewer: *Reader's Handbook,* new ed. 1898, with names and some explanation.

two dragons which had been disturbing the peace of the realm in the reign of King Lludd. They were entombed near Snowdon. They also were dug up by Vortigern and continued fighting. This last[14] myth is quite clear from history, for of the dragons one, red in colour, represented the British (Welsh) and the other, white, represented the Saxons.

The Druids represented their gods by the symbolism of the vegetable kingdom. The chief triad seems to have been oak, mistletoe and apple. Later the mistletoe became the symbol of the Messiah. It was called the Branch (*Jer* xxiii, 5) an Old Testament title of the Messiah. It was planted on a tree by a bird, symbolic of the Holy Ghost.

The Slavs at one time had three chief gods, Svantovit, Yarilo and Byelbog. Svantovit, called the white god was sometimes represented with three heads (like mediaeval figures of the Christian Trinity) or four (like images of Brahma in India). Yarilo was associated with funereal and resurrection rites. They also spoke of the three winds. With the coming of Christianity to Russia all this was abolished, but traces persisted in folk-lore.

## Buddhist Mythology

Although Buddhism originated in India, it has more or less died out there although leaving many archaeological remains. In Ceylon, Burma, Siam and Indio-China, Buddhism of the lesser vehicle (*Hinayana* or *Theravada*) still exists, whilst in the Caucasus, Mongolia, Manchuria, China, Japan, Turkestan, Ladak, Nepal, Sikkim, Bhutan, and especially Tibet the great vehicle (*Mahayana*) became very important, although now widely overshadowed in certain areas by communist governments. It is the latter form of Buddhism that has the richest mythology. In China Buddhism had to compete with, and largely mingled with, Taoism and Confucianism, in Japan with Shintoism.

[14] Vortigern, however, precedes Arthur in history.

On the altars of Buddhist temples there are three images. These are commonly said to represent the three jewels of wisdom (*tri-ratnas*) : Buddha, Dharma and Sangha. Buddha signifies initiation to the highest grade and the historical Buddha is only one of many Buddhas. Dharma is the central moral code of the Universe. Sangha (often translated *order* or *church*) is the bond of religion itself—God as love.

The philosophical systems of Buddhism are very complex, but one of the clearest accounts of the Universal Essence is given in Waddell's *Lamaism*.[15] He tells us that the three are same as one, and calls them persons, saying that they are spoken of as Tathagata and they are of one essence or substance. The idea is closely akin, if not identical with, that of the Christian Trinity. The persons, to give their best known names,[16] are (*i*) Varocana, Adi-Buddha or Vairochana who appears to be Amitabha or Amida, who presides in Heaven in Far West; (*ii*) Avalokitesvara, his son who came to the earth for the benefit of humanity, delaying his entrance to Nirvana or Heaven; and (*iii*) Kuanyin or Kwannon, generally called goddess of Mercy, but having both male and female incarnations;[17] she appears as Tara in Tibetan Lamaism.

The Taoists also have a supreme triad or Trinity and their three images appear on their altars. They are called the Three Pure Ones. They are called (*i*) Shang-ti or Yu-ti, August Supreme Emperor of Jade; (*ii*) Yu-Huang, Saviour of the World and (*iii*) Wan-chang.

The Chinese also have three star gods of happiness, rank and longevity, three aged ones, with staff, sceptre and scroll

[15] L. A. Waddell : *The Buddhism of Tibet or Lamaism*, 2nd ed. reprinted 1939.
[16] The names vary with the sect or philosophical system and are very numerous.
[17] It will be noted that Amitabha resembles the Father in Christian theology, remaining in Heaven, Avalokitesvar the Son as incarnating on earth and Kwannon the Holy Ghost as inspiring all the saints, both male and female. Some of her images resemble those of Our Lady.

and three friends Lao-tse symbolized by the plum, Confucius by the bamboo and Buddha by the pine. The last three, of course, are the founders of the three religions or cults of China, which were often blended.

## Christian Angelology

The number three is prominent in the tradition of angels passed down from Dionysius, the Aeropagite. They are classified in three circles and each of the circles in three orders.

The first circle consists of *Counsellors* and is divided into : (*i*) Seraphim represented with three pairs of crimson wings, one pair folded across the body; they carry fiery wheels studded with eyes or stars; (*ii*) Cherubim shown as winged heads of children, or children standing on wheels, hands often folded, draperies blue. (*iii*) Thrones, angels on seats covered by golden scales, their belts are of golden scales, they carry small figures of towers in their hand and stars shine on their knees.

The second circle called *Governors* consists of : (*iv*) Kyriotetes or Dominations, winged and clothed in priestly vestments, *viz.* long alb, green stole, triple crowns, they carry golden staves and the seal of God; (*v*) Dynamis or Virtues, wearing green vestments, with blue wings (feathers blue) covering breast; they carry a crown in the right hand and a censer in the left; (*vi*) Exusiai or Powers dressed as priests, but changing and scourging devils.

The third circle consists of *Ministers*. These include (*vii*) Archai or Principalities, clothed as soldiers with golden belts, with weapons or sceptres or vials and palms; (*viii*) Archangels and (*ix*) Angels, both winged and variously attired.

## Philosophy

Although it would be easy to add many other triads, major

and minor, from the world of myth, we must now pass on to some philosophical aspects of symbolism.

The dogma of the Trinity, now often regarded as a purely Christian belief, was well known in pre-Christian times. The Jews had the letter yod in a circle *or triangle* as a symbol of God, also three yods in a triangle, also three rays, as used by the Druids. Finally, some compared the letter Shin with a trident. The Jewish writer Philo (*b. circa* 40 B.C.) said[18] the Triune nature of the Deity was a secret or mystery, not to be revealed in all its parts.

Among the Greeks, Orpheus is said to have declared one God in three names. Plato[19] refers to the Divine Triad *Theos* (God), *Logos* (Word) and *Psyche* (Soul). Elsewhere he writes of Goodness, Truth and Beauty, as well known. In psychology Aristotle distinguished between rational soul, peculiar to man, the animal soul possessed by man and animals and the vegetative soul by man, animals and plants. St. Paul also had a threefold division of man: *pneuma* (spirit), *psyche* (soul) and *soma* (body). In later times such threefold classification has been advanced by as varied thinkers as Kant and Swedenborg. Among depth psychologists Freud had the threefold divisions of the Unconscious *viz.* super-ego, ego and id, whilst Jung spoke of anima, ego and persona.

Turning now to the sciences, we find modern natural science speaking of three basic physical entities, *viz.* space, time and energy. Matter, which is now regarded as a form of energy, exists in the three forms of solid, liquid and gas. Time appears to us as past, present and future.

In the occult sciences we find in astrology the basic factors of the science to be three in number, *viz.* (*i*) the *Primum Mobile,* an imaginary sphere supposed to revolve in twenty-four hours from East to West, carrying with it the planets and fixed stars, (*ii*) the *Zodiac* consisting of twelve signs, moving

[18] *De Sacrificis Abelis et Caini* quoted by Godfrey Higgins in his *Anacalypsis,* 2 vols., London, 1836.
[19] In his *Timaeus.*

as a whole, but very slowly, through the primum mobile in what has been called one Platonic Year (25,920 years) and (*iii*) the seven *Planets* moving through the zodiac at different rates. In theology the primum mobile may be said to be heaven, a symbol of God the Father, the zodiac the realm of the Son, Jesus, with the twelve signs to represent his twelve apostles,[20] whilst the seven planets represent the seven gifts[21] of the Holy Ghost (*Is* xi, 2, 3).

In alchemy there were the three principles : salt, sulphur and mercury. These were not the physical substances so named today. In fact, the last named has long been the name for quicksilver, the metal liquid at ordinary temperatures. Fortunately the alchemists had another name for mercury as a philosophical principle—*azoth*.

[20] See Chapter VI.
[21] See Chapter V.

CHAPTER III

# *Polarity*

## The Pa-Kwa

The Chinese symbol of creation, the *Pa-Kwa,* includes a circular figure divided into two equal areas, respectively black and white, and separated from one another along an S-shaped line or border, so that each area has the shape of a bent cone with rounded base.[1] The white area represents *yang,* which symbolizes the principle of light and activity and is male (positive) whilst the black area, called *yin,* represents darkness and inactivity and is female (negative). From these two everything can be derived. Around this symbol, rods arranged in threes are often shown. There are eight groups of three rods (Trigrams) in the most simple examples. Each rod is either undivided, representing yang, or divided representing yin. Every grouping of rods signifies some aspect of creation.

A similar figure to the round one is a symbol of triumph in Japan, but the black and white areas are replaced by colours, such as red and yellow. The two opposites are called *in* and *yo,* the former positive the latter negative. In Korea the figure was placed on the national flag in blue and red, surrounded by four trigrams.

The Pa-Kwa is a symbol introducing polarity. It suggests contending physical forces, like the north and south poles of

[1] The rounded figure was usually shown with eight trigrams equally distributed around it. The trigrams are each three rods, composed of complete or broken lines. According to E. J. C. Werner in *A Dictionary of Chinese Mythology* the *Pa Kua,* as he calls it, is really the eight trigrams.

the magnet and positive and negative charges in electricity. Similar in idea are the complimentary colours: red and green, orange and blue, yellow and violet, etc. Wet and dry, hot and cold are other examples. In these instances the two polar opposites are equal and opposite. There are, however, polar opposites where this does not apply, *e.g.* higher and lower, larger and smaller, health and disease and, in the moral sphere: good and evil, truth and falsity, beauty and ugliness, etc.

## The Two Pillars

As another example of an equal and opposite pair we may take the two lateral pillars of the qabalistic tree of life. The best name for these are Justice and Mercy. Indications of these are found in many myths.

There is a legend that Enoch, who was believed to be an initiate, set up two pillars, one of brick and one of stone. They were designed to survive great disasters of fire and flood, and on them both were inscribed keys to the arcana or mysteries of the antediluvian world.

The two pillars set up on either side of the temple of Solomon were called Jachin and Boaz. The first named was on the right and means 'strength', whilst the other on the left signifies 'established'. They have been said to represent the pillar of fire by night (which illuminated the path of the Israelites during their escape from Egypt) and the pillar of cloud by day (which confused the Egyptians when they tried to follow the escapers). They are, however, foreshadowed by the Egyptian columns (Taat and Tattu) which had the same significance. They were originally dedicated to Horus and Set, the rulers of the upper and lower kingdoms. The double crown of the Pharaoh also had reference to the double nature of the whole country.

In the very early culture, called the heliolithic, many kingdoms had a two-fold division. This survived in Crete where articles were often made double, *e.g.* vases with two handles. The royal symbol was the double axe, *i.e.* an axe with two blades. This has been explained by astrologers as connected with the fact that, during that period, the vernal equinox was in the sign of the Twins (Gemini).

## Heaven and Earth

Many early myths refer to the primordial gods and goddesses of heaven and earth. Usually the god is heaven and the goddess earth, as in Classical mythology. We have already referred to Uranus, god of the starry sky and Gaea the earth goddess. An exception is seen in ancient Egyptian mythology where the chief deity representing the sky was the goddess Nuit (Nut). She was shown stretched over the earth, her blue body spangled with stars. The earth is generally represented as the god Geb, called the Great Cackler, as his symbol was a goose.

The earth goddess is one of the earliest forms of the Great Mother symbol, which has been studied both by archaeologists from material remains from the past and by depth psychologists from dreams and myths. Among the earliest of known figurines are from the Aurignacean period of the old stone age (Palaeolithic). They are limestone statuettes of a female figure in which head, feet and hands are relatively small and practically formless, but the secondary sexual features of the female sex are enormously exaggerated : pudenda, buttocks, hips and breasts. Such have been called Venus-figures, but a more inappropriate name could scarcely have been chosen, seeing that Venus is the goddess of beauty and her real statues show the highest degree of harmonious proportions.

More or less similar grotesque figures have been illustrated by Erich Newmann[2] from both Palaeolithic and Neolithic times in Europe, also from pre-Colombian Peru, from Cyprus

[2] *The Great Mother, an analysis of the archetype,* trans., London, 1955.

*circa* 2500 B.C., from Mesopotamia XXIV century B.C., Phoenicia *circa* 2500 B.C., India 300–1000 B.C., Pre-dynastic Egypt, etc.

Another Great Mother symbol of late classical times has been equally misnamed. This was a monstrous female, covered with breasts. It has been quite mistakenly called Diana. But the latter was (*i*) a goddess of the moon, not the earth and (*ii*) a virgin, according to mythology.

Some of the forms of the Great Mother were of a sinister character. Ceridwen, the Keltic goddess was the possessor of a magic cauldron, and practised black magic. She was the archetype of the witch or female sorcerer. Tiamat of the Assyrians was a female dragon sometimes identified with the bitter waters or sea, conquered by Bel-Merodach or Marduk. She has been identified with the dragon, conquered by Daniel (*Dan* xiv, 25, 26). In Hindu mythology the black goddess Kali is the most terrible aspect of the wife of Shiva. She is represented as black, with four arms, carrying a sword in one and the severed head of one of the giants in another. She wears a necklace of skulls and a girdle made of the hands of dead enemies. Her eyes are red and her long tongue hangs out of her mouth. Her teeth are often shown as tusks. Several stories explain these peculiarities. Although her worship degenerated, most of the stories endeavour to show her as a protector of the gods against malevolent giants or demons. In the same way, in Tibetan Buddhism, there are fierce deities who are supposed to act as protectors of the Yellow Church.

## The Good Mother

The primitive mother is often represented with a child. She is Mary in the Christian religion, Ceres among the Romans, Demeter among the Greeks, Isis of Egypt, Mylitta of the Babylonians, Devaki (Aditi) of the Hindus, Shin-moo of the Chinese, Kwannon of the Buddhists of Japan and Tara of Tibetan Lamaism. Both Catholics and Moslems believe that both Jesus and Mary were the only human beings conceived without sin (*the immaculate conception*). This dogma must not be confused with that of *the virgin birth* which applies to Jesus, but not to his mother. Jesus in Catholic theology has two natures, being true God and true man. He is also *Alpha* and *Omega*, the Beginning and the End (*Apoc* i, 8; xxi, 6; xxii, 13).

The father of Jesus was God the Father, not the Holy Ghost as was so often wrongly supposed. Mary was filled with the Holy Ghost because she was a perfect human being, and the Holy Ghost is believed to inspire all good people, although to varying extents.

Mother and child, in a certain sense, appear to be polar opposites on the qabalistic tree of life. But there are two forms of opposition, as in astrology. There is opposition in the sense that the two are complementary, and there is opposition in the sense of antagonism; the latter is dealt with later. Here, of course, we are dealing with complete harmony. Even in early times the Mother Goddess was accompanied with a son. We have already seen that in the little known Cretan mythology there was a mother-goddess and her son-god. And in many of the myths the mother is a virgin and the son therefore of miraculous birth.

Devaki, Shin-moo, Isis, Mylitta and many others were virgin-mothers. As these are pre-Christian, their stories have been used by opponents of Christianity to discredit the Gospel story. But this carries no weight, as primitive thought often foreshadows later events of archetypal importance, like the numerous references to events in the life of Christ seen in the Old Testament.

Many of the heroes of Graeco-Roman mythology were the offspring of mortal women and immortal gods. Notable examples were Perseus, son of Danae and Jupiter; Hercules, son of Alcmena and Jupiter, Epaphus, son of Io and Jupiter; Bacchus, son of Semele and Jupiter; Orpheus, son of Calliope and Apollo and Romulus, son of Rhea Sylvia and Mars.

These can be explained by noting that the names of 'gods' were sometimes applied merely to priests of the gods.

There is, however, from the point of view of modern biology, nothing inherently impossible for virgin birth to occur, in very rare instances, even in human beings. It is well-known amongst many animals, the best known instance where it regularly occurs is the honey-bee, where the males are all produced from unfertilized eggs.[3] Possibly for that reason the bee has become the symbol of virginity.[4]

## Dualism

At one time Western writers were under the impression that the Zoroastrian religion was dualistic, *i.e.* that therein it was believed that there were two powers, one good, the other evil, more or less equal. It is now known that although the evil principle, Ahriman, is supposed to be constantly interfering with the work of the good, Ormuzd, it is the latter that is the supreme god and the evil will eventually be overcome. In fact the Zoroastrian religion is little different from the other great religions, each of which has a chief devil, often with a crowd of lesser demons. The chief of the devils is generally called Satan in the Christian religion, Shaitan or Iblis in the Moslem, Angra Mainyu or Ahriman in the Zoroastrian, Mara in the Buddhist, etc. etc. In all the great religions the power of the Evil one is strictly limited by God.

There have been, however, three considerable movements in history wherein the evil principle assumed undue importance. The first was Gnosticism. This was a pseudo-philosophical religious system especially during the first and second centuries A.D. which continued in modified forms into the

---

[3] See W. B. Crow : *A Synopsis of Biology,* Bristol, 1960, 2nd ed. 1964.

[4] In Catholic churches the candles must be composed of bee's wax.

Middle Ages. The Gnostics are sometimes regarded as Christian heretics. Their views are very varied, for there are many
different schools of thought amongst them. In any case they
reject the beliefs of the majority of Christians. They distinguished sharply between spirit and matter, believing the latter
to be essentially evil, and created by a power opposed to God
called the demiurge. They believed that marriage and pro-
creation were essentially evil as were sex and other instincts.
Some denied that Jesus was actually crucified and believed
another person or a phantom took His place on the cross.
Some even held that Sophia, the wisdom of God, went astray
and wandered into a void and dark world of Her own making.
They thought man was saved by knowledge, not by faith and
good works. They believed in powerful spirits which were
called *aeons*. These were generally supposed to be produced
from God in opposing pairs. They formed a distinct world,
called the *pleroma*, cut off from the ordinary world of matter,
the *kenoma*. Their philosophical system was based on
polarity.[5]

A second and somewhat related movement was that founded
by Manes (Mani) *circa* A.D. 216–276 in Persia. Manichaeism,
as it is called, was a fully developed dualistic cult, but borrow-
ing elements from both Christianity and Zoroastrianism. It
spread for a time into Turkestan, India and China.[6]

A third group, which has survived until recent years is that
of the Yezidis, who lived in Kurdistan, Armenia and the region
of the Caucasus, with their headquarters at Mosul in the north
of what is now Iraq. They believed the devil was one of the
fallen angels, and thought that although he had been partially
reinstated, he was much to be feared. There was no need, they
believed, to worship God, as he would never do mankind any
harm. They tried to propitiate the devil, they dared not call

[5] For further information about the Gnostics see W. B. Crow :
*A History of Magic, Witchcraft and Occultism*, London, 1968.
[6] See also *loc. cit.*, last note.

him by his true name, but called him Melek Taos, the Peacock Angel.[7]

## Lingam and Yoni

In many parts of the world, but especially in post-Vedic India the male and female external organs of sex appear as symbols. The male is called the *lingam* and the female the *yoni*, words derived from the Sanskrit. All over India the lingam is represented by a short upright pillar, carved or plain, and mounted on a stand. The latter may be rounded or oval, to represent the yoni. The figures are usually in stone, and are sometimes venerated by the country folk, who at times anoint them with milk or oil.

Many of these have been destroyed by the Moslems, not so much on the grounds of obscenity, as because the Mohammedan religion teaches the abhorrence of all images.

Some of the most famous temples in India are adorned on the outside by numerous carvings and statues of gods and mortals in sexual embrace, not always in positions regarded in the West as normal. Many of these, too, have been damaged by Moslem iconoclasts.

Temple prostitution has not been uncommon in India. According to contemporary accounts it was conducted with the utmost decorum and had nothing in common with prostitution as known in the West.

Temple prostitution was also practised in ancient Babylon and Herodotus refers to a custom there at one time wherein every woman before marriage had to repair to the temple and act as a prostitute at least once in her lifetime, but this has been doubted.

That the union of the sexes was regarded as a symbol of the union of the spiritual with the material is undoubted. Even in the Christian religion there are many signs of this. In the Old Testament the *Canticle of Canticles* or *Song of Solomon*

[7] *loc. cit.*, last note.

celebrates the high mysteries of the happy union of Christ and His spouse, who is the Church. Nuptial symbolism is also seen in *Isias* (*Isaiah*) lxii, 5, in *Osee* (*Hosea*) ii, 14 and especially in many places in the last book of the New Testament, where the Church is represented as the Bride of the Lamb, *Apocalypse* xii, l.

In the Catholic Church marriage is one of the seven sacraments. Earthly marriage is supposed to reflect the heavenly union of Christ and His Church. The consecration of a nun is also regarded as the union of an individual soul with Christ and the ceremony has considerable similarity to an earthly marriage.

## Polarity in Astrology and Alchemy

In Astrology the idea of polar opposites is frequently met with. Some of the planets are harmonious with one another, some are inharmonious. Some of the aspects are supposed to be fortunate, some unfortunate. But polarity is most clearly shown in the Zodiac from the fact that some signs are permanently in opposition to one another. Opposition here represents not only an adverse influence but also sometimes partnership. Aries is opposite to Libra, Taurus to Scorpio, Gemini to Sagittarius, Cancer to Capricorn, Leo to Aquarius and Virgo to Pisces.

A glance at alchemical diagrams will convince anyone that polarity played a large part in that subject. Sun and moon, king and queen, man and woman, opposing birds and beasts and a figure half male and half female, the alchemical hermaphrodite, often occur.

# CHAPTER IV

# The Elements

## Canopic Jars

Among the numerous antiquities from ancient Egypt, jars, with the lid adorned with the figure of a head, are found. These are known as Canopic Jars from a belief that a certain mythological Spartan named Canopus was buried at a place called after him and was figured in the form of a jar. However, the jars of this type came into use as early as the sixth dynasty for receiving the intestines and other viscera of the dead. At first the Jars were represented with human heads, but later (eighteenth dynasty) received images of the four sons of the God Horus. These were (*i*) Amset or Mestha, who retained the human head and in whose Jar the liver was deposited, (*ii*) Hapi, who had the head of a baboon and whose jar contained the lungs, (*iii*) Duamutef with the head of a dog, whose jar contained the stomach and (*iv*) Qebehsenuf, with the head of a falcon, the jar containing the intestines.[1] The viscera were often mummified or preserved in some way, but the most interesting thing is that it appears to have been the practice to place them around the last resting place of the mummy and at the four cardinal points : North, South, East and West. Amset was placed in the West, Hapi in the East, Duamutef in the South and Qebehsenuf in the North. Canopic Jars remained in use until the twenty-sixth dynasty.

In funeral tablets showing the Judgement of the Dead, four creatures resembling the figures on the Canopic Jars

[1] The particular viscera contained in each jar are differently indentified by different investigators and may have varied over the long period during which this custom was in use.

appear and are said to be mediating with Osiris, the Judge of the dead, on behalf of the deceased.

It is a very curious thing that the native cultures of America have very close resemblances to that of Egypt, in spite of the vast distance in between, and the Mayas of Central America had gods of the four quarters called *Bacabs*, to each of which was assigned a particular colour.

A reminiscence in folk lore among Christian people may have survived in the ancient rhyme invoking the four Evangelists to bless the bed before retiring to sleep.

The truth is that almost all the great religions had four important spirits, called saints, gods or mythological creatures of some kind ruling the four quarters of the heavens, the four directions of space and the four elements. In Chinese Buddhist temples two great wooden images greet one on entry on each side. These are the four deva-kings, derived from Hinduism. They are called To-wen, Chi-kwo, Tseng-chang and Kwang-mu. But their Hindu names are Vaishramana, Dhritarashtra, Virudhaka and Virupaksha.[2] In Chinese art they are represented by

(*i*) the blue or green dragon, chief of scaly creatures, corresponding with the season of spring, the element wood, the viscera liver and gall bladder and the Eastern point of the compass;

(*ii*) the red bird, chief of feathery creatures corresponding with the summer season, the fiery element, the heart and large intestines and the Southern point of the compass;

(*iii*) the white tiger, chief of hairy creatures corresponding with the season of autumn, the airy element, the lungs and small intestine and the Western point of the compass;

(*iv*) the black tortoise, chief of shelly creatures, corresponding with winter, with the watery element, the kidneys and urinary bladder and the Northern point of the compass.

[2] J. Edkins: *Chinese Buddhism,* London, 2nd ed. Preface dated 1879.

In Japan the four guardian-kings are identical with those of China and India. They are (*i*) Jikoku, the green-faced who protects the East and is a warrior. He carries a sword in his left hand, an ossuary in his right and is sometimes shown trampling a demon under foot. He is identical with Dhritar-ashtra. (*ii*) Zocho, the white-faced, who is also a warrior, carrying a sword and buckler, protects the South. He is identical with Virudhaka. (*iii*) Komoku, the red-faced, who protects the West, carries a spear or brush and a book. He is identical with Virupaksha. (*iv*) Tamon or Tamoten, the blue, holding a sceptre in his left hand and small ossuary in the form of a pagoda in the right, rules the North. He is identical with Vaishramana. He is also sometimes called Bishamon, but strictly the latter is one of the seven gods of happiness.

The Hindus also have eight gods relating to the directions of space, or even nine, as will be described later.

## Beasts and Evangelists

In the wonderful vision of the prophet Ezekiel (*Ez* i, 4–28) representing the likeness of the glory of the Lord (*Ez* ii, 1) four living creatures were seen. These are called somewhat strangely the four beasts (from a Greek word meaning a living creature) supporting the throne of God. They are also referred to in *Eccl* xlix, 10 in the Old Testament. They also reappear in the New Testament (*Apoc* iv, 6). The first was like a lion, the second like a calf, the third like a man and the fourth like an Eagle (*Apoc* iv, 7). These four living creatures play an important part in the symbolism of both the Jewish and Christian religion. So mysterious did the Jews regard them that, according to St. Jerome, only students above the age of thirty were allowed to read Ezekiel's vision.

Among the Christians the four living creatures have been ascribed to the four Evangelists. Just as the living creatures uphold the throne of God, so the four Evangelists uphold the

Christian Faith. As is well known they are shown, in pictures of the crucified Christ, one at each of, or between, the four arms of the cross. It is said that they symbolize the particular Gospels. Thus Matthew is represented as a man because in his Gospel he dwells particularly upon the manhood of Christ. Mark is shown as a lion, as this powerful animal is not easily slain, so he symbolizes by his powerful vitality the resurrection of Christ, which is most fully dealt with in St. Mark's Gospel. Luke is symbolized as the ox, as this was the chief of sacrificial animals as shown by Apis in Egypt, and St. Luke deals most fully with the priesthood and sacrifice of Christ. John is shown as an eagle as his Gospel pays somewhat less attention to earthly matters and deals with the airy realm of the Logos doctrine and the mysteries.

Quite in harmony with the preceding we find the four living creatures representing four events in the life of Christ : (*i*) the man representing the incarnation or birth as a human being; (*ii*) the ox, as a sacrifice, representing the crucifixion; (*iii*) the lion, as an animal that can revive after being apparently slain, symbolizing the resurrection; and (*iv*) the eagle, as a creature that flies high into the sky, symbolizing the ascension of Jesus into Heaven.

## Astrological Allusions

Many authors have identified the four living creatures with the four fixed signs of the Zodiac. The word Zodiac is said to be derived from 'the circle of the beasts', although not all are now animal figures. The four fixed signs are as follows. The man is Aquarius, the water-pourer, represented by a human figure pouring water and astrologers will be familiar with the belief that this sign is associated with human brotherhood. The ox is Taurus, the sign of the bull, and rules the priesthood. The lion is Leo, the royal sign, which signifies kingship and nobility. The eagle, taking the place of Scorpio, is said to have taken the place of that sign in some early versions of the Zodiac, and represents the prophetic office.

If the figure of the incarnate God on the cross be placed on a diagram of the Zodiac, with the mid-line of His head between the signs Aries the ram and Pisces the fishes, then the four fixed signs come between the four limbs of the cross. The reason for choosing Aries and Pisces is that the former represents Christ as the Lamb of God, whilst *Piscis*, meaning a fish, is an ancient symbol of the Lord under the name *Ichthys*, the Greek word for *fish* often abbreviated to IHS in ecclesiastical symbolism.

Among the Persians, before the time of Christ, four stars were near the equinoxes and the solstices. They were (*i*) in the bull, Taurus, (*ii*) the lion, Leo and (*iii*) the scorpion, Scorpio, and one (*iv*) was in the fishes, Pisces, but owing to the great size of the constellation of that name, it overlapped into the sign Aquarius. However, because of the movement known as the Precession of the Equinoxes (which involves the Solstices as well), they have now moved backwards into or nearly into the next sign. They are as follows : (*i*) Aldebaran, the Bull's Eye (south or left eye) a single star of pale rose colour, called Watcher of the East, marking in those ancient days the position of the Vernal Equinox, but now in Gemini 8° 40′; (*ii*) Regulus or Cor Leonis, the Heart of the Lion, a double star, the components of which are white and indigo, called Watcher of the South and marking the Summer Solstice, but now in Leo 28° 43′; (*iii*) Antares or Cor Scorpii, the Heart of the Scorpion, the first name meaning rival of Mars or Ares, a double star, the components being ruby red and emerald green, called Watcher of the West, marking the Autumnal Equinox, but now in Scorpio 8° 39′; (*iv*) Fomalhaut, meaning the Mouth of the Fish (Southern Fish), which is double, reddish white with a very small bluish white companion, and is called Watcher of the North and once marking the Winter Solstice, but now in Pisces 2° 44′.

In astrology there is also an allusion to the four elements, of which the material universe was believed to be composed. The planets and the zodiacal signs were each assigned to one of the four. Saturn was an earthy planet, he ruled Capricorn which was earthy and Aquarius which was airy. Jupiter was fiery,[3] he ruled Sagittarius which was fiery and Pisces which was watery. Mars was always fiery, he ruled Aries which was fiery and Scorpio which was watery. The Sun was of course also fiery and he ruled Leo, a fiery sign. Venus was a watery planet, but she ruled Taurus which was earthy and Libra which was airy. Mercury was airy and ruled the airy sign Gemini and the earthy sign Virgo. The Moon, of course, was watery and ruled the watery sign Cancer.

## Alchemical Allusions

It is sometimes supposed that the four elements of alchemy and of early science in general were merely the primitive version of the chemical elements of today, and have been superseded by the latter. Nothing could be further from the truth. The four elements persisted in science long after numerous chemical elements had been discovered, as shown in the great work of Oken.[4] Indeed, the idea is still useful today in natural science for they represent four states of matter and energy: earth being the solid state, water the liquid, air the gaseous and fire free forms of energy, it being now admitted by chemists and physicists that matter and energy are essentially one. However, the fourfold classification applied in mediaeval times to other than physical phenomena and in recent times has entered the science of depth psychology. In fact it may be said that the idea of the four elements is valid upon all planes.

Already in the works of Hippocrates (460–377 B.C.) the four temperaments are distinguished: Sanguine, choleric, melancholic and phlegmatic, characterized by the predominance of one of the four humours: blood, bile, black bile and phlegm.

---

[3] To Jupiter however the ether was especially assigned.
[4] *Elements of Physiophilosophy*, trans., London, 1847.

The last named has been identified with lymph. We still speak of individuals being sanguine, from the Latin word *sanguis* which not only refers to blood, but also to life and vigour. The sanguine temperament corresponds with the element fire. A bilious individual nowadays is regarded as an invalid, but it does not need much imagination to understand the bilious or choleric temperament, the word *chole* being a Greek word for bile. It corresponds with the element air. Black bile is *melagcholia* in Greek and is the melancholic temperament corresponding with the element earth. The phlegmatic temperament is well known. It corresponds with the element water. These temperaments were widely accepted by the alchemists, many of whom were also physicians.

In more modern times a number of authors have adopted or invented a four-fold human classification. These often strongly suggest the aforesaid alchemical ideas. The French physiologist Halle in 1797 suggested the four types should be adominal, muscular, respiratory, nervous. Rostan, a French physician in 1828, had much the same types and called them digestive, muscular, respiratory and cerebral. Carus, German obstetrician and philosopher in 1852, spoke of phlegmatic, athletic, asthenic and cerebral types. Virenius, a Russian, in 1904 made them correspond to the four main types of tissues, calling them connective, muscular, epithelial and nervous. The Frenchman Sigaud in 1906 went back to calling them digestive, muscular, respiratory and cerebral, whilst in 1917 the American R. W. Mills coined the terms sthenic, hypersthenic, hyposthenic and asthenic.

Most of the preceding were based on bodily or physiological conditions, although, of course, body and mind do correspond to a large extent. In 1920 the Swiss analytical psychologist C. G. Jung announced in addition to his well-known idea of extravert and introvert, four modifying types that clearly correspond with the alchemical: feeling (corresponding with water), sensation (earth) thinking (air) and intuition (fire). It is significant that later on Jung discovered a psychological meaning for alchemy, although he had previously no dealings with the subject.

The quadruple classification can also be seen in the classification of social groups from the earliest times. In ancient Egypt the Othphto were the secluded or monastic orders, with links to modern freemasonry, corresponding with water, the Bachano were the hired temple servers, corresponding with earth, the Soteno were the mayors and magistrates, corresponding with air, whilst the Nouto were wholly engaged in sacrificial duties corresponding with fire. Even more clearly does the classification apply to the caste system of India, the Vaishya, merchants and landowners, corresponding with water, the Shudra or labourers with earth, the Kshatriya or warriors and governors, with air and the Brahmin which included priests and teachers, with fire. In mediaeval Europe we can see these correspond with (i) merchants, (ii) agricultural and other workers, (iii) kings, nobility and the knighthood and (iv) the priesthood.

In history almost all nations have had a tradition of the four ages of the world: (i) the Golden Age of primitive harmony, when man lived on the fruits of the earth, corresponding with the Old Stone Age or Palaeolithic; (ii) the Silver Age which began with the introduction of agriculture, corresponding with the New Stone Age or Neolithic; (iii) the Copper or Bronze Age when the shield and helmet were introduced and fighting became common; and (iv) the Iron Age, when complete sets of armour became necessary, all sorts of weapons were introduced and conflict became universal.

## Elementals

In mediaeval Europe there were many legends of non-human beings called in occult books *elemental spirits* or *elementals*. They were of a considerably lower order of life than the angels, nor must they be confused with the spirits of dead human beings or ghosts, which have been designated *elementaries.* There are also frequent references to what appear to be the same as the elementals in the pagan mythology of many ancient nations, *i.e.* to creatures of a lower order of being than the gods, which appear in many myths. Although often mischievous, the elementals are not malicious and must not be mistaken for devils. Indeed it was said that Adam, before the Fall, had them as helpers, and that, by certain ceremonies, human beings could establish good relations with them. It was even maintained that marriages could be arranged between men or women on the one hand and elementals on the other and that offspring could be produced. Stories about such remind one of the mediaeval tales of *incubi* and *succubi*.[5]

The elementals were usually said to be mortal, although they lived much longer than human beings.

There were four great classes of elementals, corresponding with the four elements, as follows :

1. The *gnomes* are the elementals of the element Earth. They live in underground caves, frequently at a great depth. They were sometimes encountered in mines and the German miners called them *kobolds*. Some identify them with *goblins* or *lutins*, especially when they visit human abodes. The females of these elementals are called *gnomides*. Both males and females are usually much smaller than men and women. The ruler of the gnomes was called Gob. They especially influence people of melancholic temperament and they are assigned to the compass-point of the North.

2. The elementals pertaining to water are called *undines*. These are the *water nymphs* of classical mythology and the *mermaids* and *mermen* of mediaeval legend. Some lived in the sea (*Oceanides, Nereides*), some in fresh-water (*Naiades*). They are usually represented as human above the waist, but fish-like below. The males are much rarer than the females. The ruler

[5] For further details of the latter see pp. 248–250 of the present author's *A History of Magic, Witchcraft and Occultism*, London, 1968.

of the Undines is called Necksa. They influence people of a phlegmatic or lymphatic temperament. They are assigned to the compass point of the West.

3. The elementals pertaining to the air are called *sylphs*. They are the *fairies* of mediaeval stories. In Moslem legends of King Solomon they are apparently described as *birds*, for they fly about in the air and in other ways are portrayed as bird-like. The ruler of the sylphs is called Paralda. They influence people of a bilious temperament. They are assigned to the compass point of the East.

4. The *salamanders* are the elementals of fire. They are most fully described in the Moslem legends recorded in the famous *Thousand and One Nights*. Therein they are called *djinn* or *jinn* (singular *djinni* or *jinni*). They are said to be composed of smokeless fire, in contrast to the angels, who were made of light. There are no less than five subdivisions of this group. The jinn mostly live in the distant country of Qaf, a realm surrounding all the rest of the world. But among men they are found on the sea shore, the banks of rivers and in ruins and deserted places. They fly rapidly through the air, but many are constantly being killed by shooting stars. Apart from this they are said to live for several centuries. Their ruler was called Djinn. They influenced people of a sanguine temperament. They are assigned to the compass point of the South.

## The Four Gods

In most mythic systems there is a god of fire, a god of the air or winds, a god of water or the seas and an earth goddess. We only have space to give a few examples.

In the classics, Vulcan (*Lat.*) or Hephaestus (*Gk.*) was the god of fire. He is represented as a blacksmith, wearing a leather apron and cap and holding a hammer. He was supposed to be lame. He was not only a great worker in iron and bronze, but also in gold and silver. He made the sickle for

Ceres or Demeter, arrows for Apollo and Diana (Artemis), the sword of Perseus and other wonderful objects. He even made human figures and those of animals. He causes volcanoes, escapes of burning gases from the earth and the boiling up of hot springs.

Agni is the fire-god of the Hindus. He carries a fiery torch and rides in a chariot drawn by red horses. He has an assistant called Twashtri, whilst Vulcan is assisted by the Cyclopes. In Egypt the chief fire-god was Ptah, represented by a deformed dwarf. Like Vulcan he participated in creation. In Babylonia he was Gibil, and was also god of metal workers. Among the Phoenicians he was Kushor or Kusor. Among the Zoroastrians the genius of fire was Atar, one of the Yazatas or celestial beings. Among the Norse he was Loki, who possessed magical powers. The Slavs called him Ogon. He was even known in the New World; the Aztecs for instance called him Xiuhtecuhtli.

In Greek mythology Aeolus is the deity best representing the air. He was god of the winds, which he confined in bags, only allowing them out when he decided each could blow. He was thus responsible for storms and hurricanes. Another story ascribes to him the invention of sails.

In Egypt the god Shu represented the atmosphere. He was said to separate the heaven goddess Nuit and the earth-god Geb. In Babylonia, Adad was the god of winds and storms. The Phoenicians had a god of the atmosphere called Aer. The Zoroastrians had a Yazata or celestial being, called Vita, ruling the atmosphere. The Hindu god of the winds was called Vayu.

As regards the watery element, Neptune (*Lat.*) or Poseidon (*Gk.*) was the chief of the waters in the classic era and was ruler of the sea. He could raise up islands and also caused earthquakes. He also ruled over freshwaters, *viz.* lakes, ponds, rivers and even fountains. He is pictured holding his trident, crowned with seaweed, drawn in a car by sea-horses, surrounded by numerous nymphs, fishes and sometimes a few whales. The deities of the sea were very many, of course, but he was the chief. In ancient Egypt he was represented by Canopus or Hapi. In the Babylonian system he was Oannes, a culture-hero, represented as half man above, and half fish below. In Phoenician myth the same figure is called Dagon. Among the Zoroastrians the celestial being presiding over water was Apo. The Norse god of the sea was Aegir.

The great earth-mother was known in prehistoric times, from rough stone images. In the classics she is Terra or Tellus (*Lat.*) or Gaea (*Gk.*). In Egyptian mythology the earth deity is male, but is called Geb or Gae. But there is an earlier (pre-dynastic) mother goddess called Mehueret. In Hinduism the earth-goddess is called Prithivi. In Babylon she was Ashtart or Asherah. In the New World the earth-goddess is met with as Tlazolteotl or Coatlicue among the Aztecs. The last named is described as serpent-skirted. A goddess entwined by a snake was found as far away as ancient Crete and Syria, and was even known in the early days of Greece.[6] The many-breasted so-called 'Diana of the Ephesians' supposed to be mentioned in the New Testament (*Acts* xix, 27–35) and known from images as late as the second century A.D. is another great earth goddess and is nothing to do with the virginal moon goddess Diana of the Romans, Artemis of the Greeks.

Hertha or Nerthus was the Norse earth-mother and from the former name is derived our English word earth. She was Danu or Anu of the Irish Kelts and Keridwen or Ceridwen of the Welsh. The offspring of Danu, called the Tuatha de Danann, were the fifth body of invaders that conquered Ireland. They were afterwards themselves overcome by the Milesians from Spain, but many legends remained of their exploits.

## The Four Treasures

The Tuatha de Danann were supposed to come from four

[6] See figures in E. Neumann : *The Great Mother,* trans., London, 1955.

islands in the ocean, reputed to be remains of the former continent of Atlantis. They brought with them four treasures, as follows:

1. From Finias, which was the southern of the four islands, came the sword of Nuda, king of the Tuatha de Danann. Nuda was identified with the ancient British king Ludd, who has given his name to Ludgate in London.

2. From Gorias, which was the eastern of the four islands, came the lance of Lugh or Lugus, who was the grandson of Danu and identical with the Welsh Llew.

3. From Murias, the most western of the four islands, came the cauldron of Dagda, another king of the Tuatha de Danann. This has been identified with the cauldron of Keridwen and other magical cauldrons in Keltic and Norse mythology.

4. The stone of destiny was from Falias, the northern isle. This has been identified as the stone mentioned in the Old Testament (*Gen* xxviii, 18, 22) brought by the prophet Jeremiah to Ireland, where his tomb is shown in Loch Erne.[7] The stone was subsequently taken to Scotland in A.D. 502 by Fergus and he and his successors, thirty-four in all, were crowned on it. In 1296 Edward I of England removed it to Westminster and had the present Coronation Chair made for it. The prophecy that wherever it should be a Scot should reign was apparently fulfilled at the Union.

It is obvious that these four treasures correspond with the four elements and the four suits of the Tarot: fire or swords, air or rods, cups or water and discs or earth.

These four naturally occur very frequently in myth and legend. For example:

1. The black stone (Hajaru'l Aswad) in the Kabah at Mecca, the central object of Islamic pilgrimages; the disc or *Chakra* of Vishnu, of the Hindu religion; the wheel of the law

[7] For further details see W. B. Crow: The Symbolism of the Coronation, *Mysteries of the Ancients*, 15, London, 1944.

of the Buddhists; the white stone of the Apocalypse of St. John (ii, 17); the philosopher's stone of the Alchemists; the stone talisman of Abraxas of the Gnostics; the serpent-stone of the *Mabinogion* of the Welsh, which gave untold gold to those who held it in their hands.

2. The cup of Helios, the sun-god, made by Vulcan; the *cornucopia* from the horn of Amalthaea, the goat-goddess in the milk of whom the infant Jupiter was nourished, it furnished unlimited food for the attendant nymphs, the magic cauldron from Arawn, King of the Underworld which went to the court of King Arthur, it could multiply food put into it one hundred times; the cauldron of Keridwen that gave poetic inspiration, and knowledge of past and future; the cauldron called Tyrnog Diwrnach, of British myth, that boiled only for the brave; the cauldron of Dagda, already mentioned, it was filled with water and fading light, the latter no doubt a reference to the astral world; the cauldron of Bran which regenerated warriors slain in battle; the cauldron of Manannan, the Irish god of the sea, which figures in the legend of Cuchulainn; the well of Mimir in Norse mythology for a draught of which Odin was ready to leave as a pledge one of his eyes; the three cauldrons of Suttung, the giant in Norse mythology, one of which contained the blood of Quasir (or Kvasir) the wisest of men, mixed with mead, on which the Aesir, the high gods were sustained in wisdom and immortality; the cup of Djemscheed, filled with the elixir of life and reflecting in its depths everything that happens in the world.

3. Rods are represented by the magic wands of all magicians, by the croziers of bishops, by the spears of knights and the sceptres of kings. A famous example was the emerald sceptre of Prester John. Other examples are the spear of Achilles which could both kill and cure; the spear of King Arthur, called Rone and the caduceus of Mercury in classical mythology.

4. Swords in legends often have names and are too numerous to list. Among the most noteworthy were: the sword of

Perseus, made by Vulcan, Excalibar and Caliburn, the swords of King Arthur (the first named he pulled out of the stone, thus proving himself rightful king of Britain, the second a magical sword from the Lady of the Lake); Balmung was the sword of Siegfried, made by Wieland, the Norse Vulcan; Curtana or sword of mercy of Edward the Confessor, still used in the English coronation.

Another representation of the four is seen in the Christian legends of the Holy Grail. They were called the *hallows* and they often appear together in manifestations of the Grail. They were as follows:

1. The Grail[8] itself, which was the chalice used by Jesus at the Last Supper, and afterwards used by Joseph of Arimathen to collect the blood of Jesus whilst He was on the cross.

2. The platter or dish, said to have carried the paschal lamb at the Last Supper.

3. The spear of the centurion Longinus, with which he wounded the side of Jesus, whilst He was on the cross.

4. The sword of David, passed to Solomon his son and belonging to Jesus as King of the Jews.

It is curious to note that the equivalents of the four hallows appear in the ceremonies of the Catholic Church. The chalice and paten used in the Mass, both in the Eastern and Western rites, of course, are obviously the same as the Grail and the paschal dish. The Eastern rite also makes use of a small spear for cutting the bread before consecration, and this, to judge from the wording of the accompanying prayers, is undoubtedly used to represent the spear used to wound Christ on the cross. Lastly, in the Western rite the sword, although not used in the Mass, is placed in the hand of a candidate for the office of Exorcist, one of the necessary stages leading to the priesthood.

[8] For further details see W. B. Crow: *A History of Magic, Witchcraft and Occultism,* London, 1968.

## The Winds

The four winds of the Ancient Egyptians resembled the four gods of the cardinal points in having animal heads and may have been identical with the canopic images. Among the Greeks and Romans the winds were also personified. They were confined in caves in the island-kingdom of Aeolia, where they were ruled by Aeolus, god of the winds. He regulated their access to the world of men with the utmost severity, since should they blow in a lawless fashion, chaos would result. Even so they were often the cause of dangerous storms.

No less than eight winds were recognized. Four of them came from the four cardinal points, north, south, east and west. But four others with different qualities came in between, *viz.* north-east and north-west, south-east and south-west.

Boreas was the North Wind. Like all the others, he was winged. He had white hair, was often covered in cloud and often brought rain, snow and frost. He was fabled to have a castle in the far north, built of snow crystals.

Notus or Auster was the South Wind. He was represented as an old man, with dark wings and brought heavy rain.

Apeliotes, sometimes confused with Eurus, was the East Wind. He was represented as a young man with long hair, carrying fruits of many kinds.

Zephyrus or Favonius was the West Wind. He also was represented as a young man, with only a loose mantle, carrying flowers.

Caecias or Kaikas, also known as Aquilo, was the North-East Wind and is represented as an old man carrying a round shield. He was especially associated with hail, and the shield may be meant as a protection therefrom.

Argestes, Corus or Sciron was the North-West Wind, bitterly cold and dry in winter, scorchingly hot in summer. He is represented as a man with a languid appearance carrying a pot filled with ashes to show the dryness of the wintry, and the burning heat of the summery quality of this wind.

Eurus or Volturnus was the South-East Wind. He is represented as a morose old man, covered in a mantle.

Africus or Libs was the South-West Wind and was represented as a young man with dark wings, emptying a jar of water or as an old man surrounded by clouds.

In Hindu mythology some of the most important gods are called *loka-palas* as presiding over the four cardinal points and the four points between the latter. When represented as such they are shown seated on eight male elephants and it is sometimes said that these elephants are the loka-palas or guardians of the world. Each elephant has his consort or female.

Indra, god of the firmament or atmosphere is the loka-pala of the East; Agni, god of fire, of the south-east, Yama, god of death, of the south, Surya, god of the sun, of the south-west, Varuna, god of the sea and waters, of the west; Vayu, god of the wind, of the north-west, Kubera or Kuvera, god of wealth and of the underworld, of the north; Soma, god of the elixir of life and of the moon, of the north-east.

Taoist mythology of China includes a group termed the *eight immortals*. They are mortals who have attained immortality suddenly on account of their good deeds. Their names have been transliterated variously. Here is one version (*i*) Li Tieh-Kuai, who took on the body of a beggar and is shown with a crutch and carries a gourd supposed to contain drugs, being a patron of pharmacists; (*ii*) Chung-Li Chuan, carrying a fan and supposed to be an alchemist; (*iii*) Lan Tsai-Ho, sometimes considered to be an hermaphrodite, represented as a street-singer or a gardener, carrying fruit; (*iv*) Chang-Kuo Lao, an old man who travelled on a magical donkey, which, when not in use could be folded up like a piece of paper; he was the patron of artists, carrying a tabor or small drum, with drumstick; (*v*) Ho Hsien-ku, a maiden, carrying the lotus or the peach of immortality; (*vi*) Lu Tung-Pin, a dragon-slayer, carrying a sword and what has been described as a fly-whisk, a Taoist symbol of ability to fly to heaven; (*vii*) Han Hsiang-

Tzu, carrying a flute as patron of musicians; and (*viii*) Tsao Kuo-Chiu, a royal personage who became a hermit, he carries a tablet of admission to court in his hand.

The number eight figures in several ways in Chinese symbolism. Of the numerous gods worshipped in China, eight were regarded as having been venerated from the most ancient times. Then there is the noble eight-fold path of the Buddhists, the eight-fold division of the relics of Buddha and their enshrining in eight great caityas[9] in diverse parts of the world,[10] the eight symbols shown on figures of Buddha's footprints, the eight glorious offerings,[11] the eight precious things[12] and the eight mystic trigrams of the Pa Kua or Pa-kwa,[13] each consisting of three rods which can either be continuous or interrupted by a gap ($2^3 = 8$).

## Ether

In Hindu mythology, as we have seen, the four elements were recognized, each ruled over by the corresponding god: Taijas or Tejas, fire, ruled by Agni; Anila, air, ruled by Vayu; Jala or Apu, water, ruled by Varuna and Bhu; earth, ruled by Prithivi. But there was a fifth element Akasha, ether, vibra-

[9] Dome-shaped funereal monuments.

[10] The eight places were alleged to be : (*i*) the site of Buddha's death at Kusinagara in Assam; (*ii*) Mount Potala in Southern Tibet; (*iii*) the mythical kingdom of Shambhala in Central Asia; (*iv*) the fairy-land of Udyana in Western Tibet; (*v, vi* and *vii*) three mountains of Manjusri, the god of Wisdom in Northern China; (*viii*) Lhasa, the home of the Dalai Lama.

[11] These were : (*i*) golden fish, symbolizing faith; (*ii*) white umbrella, signifying authority; (*iii*) conch or shell trumpet, signifying victory; (*iv*) knotted band, signifying longevity; (*v*) canopy or banner, signifying sovereignty; (*vi*) reliquary, honouring the dead; (*vii*) lotus, symbolizing purity and (*viii*) chakra or wheel of the law, represented by a sort of disc.

[12] These were : (*i*) the pearl; (*ii*) musical instrument, (*iii*) mirror; (*iv*) coin; (*v*) leaf of *Artemisia*; (*vi*) rhinoceros horn cups; (*vii*) jade gong; (*viii*) two books representing learning and wisdom.

[13] See page 39.

tion or radiation, ruled by Indra. The addition of this element brought the five elements into line with the five senses: touch or common sensation being earth; taste, water; smell, air; fire, vision; and ether, sound.

It is of interest that, far away in time and space, in mediaeval Europe, among the alchemists, there developed the idea of a mysterious fifth element, called the Quintessence. This was probably derived from India, however, as it was spoken of by Pythagoras, who is alleged to have travelled to the East.

Among the very many symbols arranged in fives we may cite the five elements of the ancient Chinese: earth, water, wood, metal and fire, the five orders of architecture among the Greeks and Romans: Doric, Ionic, Corinthian, Tuscan and Composite; the five regular geometrical solids of Plato: tetrahedron, hexahedron, octahedron, dodecahedron and icosahedron, each bounded by similar, equal and regular surfaces.

Among the Christians a certain amount of symbolism surrounds the centre and four arms of the cross, and the five wounds of Christ.

CHAPTER V

# *The Planets*

## Planets and Stars

In Europe in the Middle Ages astrology flourished[1] and depended upon the movements of the seven planets in the zodiac and the twelve houses. The planets, in order of rapidity of motion were reckoned to be, beginning with the swiftest: the moon, Mercury, Venus, the sun, Mars, Jupiter and Saturn. The sun and moon were called luminaries, but they were always treated as planets.

In European astrology the moon is female. She represents the mother and everything pertaining to birth and home life. Mercury is male. (Some say hermaphrodite.) He represents the child or the youth and everything pertaining to intelligence, knowledge, education and trade. Venus is female. She represents the lover or wife, and everything pertaining to the fine arts. The sun is male. He represents the hero and everything pertaining to honour and glory. Mars is male. He represents the warrior or husband and everything pertaining to war or conflict. Jupiter is male. He represents the priest and everything connected with space, custom, law, religion and wisdom. Saturn is a eunuch. He represents the father and old people in general. He is connected with pain, disease, decay and death and everything pertaining to time. Numerous works on astrology are available to those wishing to know more of astrological symbolism. Here we can give only a brief indication.

The mediaeval astrologers sometimes made use of what were

[1] See W. B. Crow: *A History of Magic, Witchcraft and Occultism,* London, 1968.

called the Dragon's Head and the Dragon's Tail. These were derived from Hindu astrology where they are called Rahu (the head) and Kethu (the tail) and are called *shadow-planets* and supposed to cause eclipses. They are really the ascending node (the head) and the descending node (the tail) of the moon. They cannot be considered as true planets and this, in fact, has long been known among the initiated.

The Hindus have seven planets which are precisely the same as the European set. They also rule the same day of the week. Thus Ravi is the sun and rules Sunday, Chandra the moon, who rules Monday, Mangala corresponding to Mars ruling Tuesday ( = Mardi = Mars' day in French), Budha[2] ruling Wednesday ( = Mercredi; Mercury's day in French), Vrihaspati (Brihaspati) ruling Thursday, Sukra ruling Friday (Vendredi: Venus day in French) and Sani, Saturday. Unlike the Western system both Chandra, the moon and Sukra (Venus) are regarded as males like all the others. The equivalents in Teutonic mythology have sometimes been used in English, *e.g.* Tuisco (Tuesday) Woden (Mercury), Wednesday, Thor (Jupiter) Thursday and Freya (Venus) Friday.

The planets appear to move so rapidly because they are, compared with the so-called fixed stars, much nearer the earth. The very word *planet* is derived from this great ability to move. The fixed stars, of course, also move, but are so far away that their movement is imperceptible, except over very long periods.

There seems to have been an arcane teaching[3] that the seven planets of our solar system were only a lower reflex of the seven fixed stars known as the Pleiades.

The Pleiades were supposed to be the seven daughters of Atlas and Pleione, or rather the seven stars which were named after them. They were as follows: Maia, whose star was the

---

[2] Not to be confused with Buddha, the ninth incarnation of Krishna.

[3] E. C. Farnsworth, *The Arcane Science*, Portland, Maine, U.S.A., 1913.

most luminous, and who was the mother of the god Mercury (Hermes) by Jupiter (Zeus) the king of the gods, Electra and Taygeta who also had children by Jupiter, Alcyone and Celaeno who had children by Neptune and Sterope who was mother of a child by Mars; finally there was Merope, whose star was almost invisible, as she married a mere mortal, Sisyphus, King of Corinth. In India, Babylon, Persia, China, Europe and even among the natives of Peru and Australia the Pleiades were of immense importance in folk-lore, and somehow they gained a high place in the stellar mythology. They were on a higher octave, but corresponded with the planets. It must be noted that the Pleiades group really contains a vast number of stars, of which only seven were of great importance, just as, in the solar system, the planets Uranus, Neptune and Pluto, not to mention all the planetoids, play no part in tradition, being unknown in ancient times.[4]

But beyond the Pleiades, and on a still higher octave were the seven stars of Ursa Major, the plough or Great Bear. The latter name was used all over the world, even by the American Indians, in spite of the fact that the constellation in no way resembles a bear, but is a quadrangle of four stars with three others forming a long tail, a part of the body which no bear possesses. The Greeks said it was the maiden Callisto, seduced by Zeus, king of the gods, and transformed into a bear by Hera, queen of the gods, in a fit of jealousy, and placed in the heavens with her son by Zeus. The son Arcas was transformed into Ursa Minor, the lesser bear, and it is in the latter that the pole star Polaris is situated. The Chinese called the constellation the Holy Mount of God or words to that effect.

In Ursa Major, the great bear, the seven chief stars are arranged four in the quadrangle and three in the long tail. In Western astrology they have Arabic names, as is usual, but the Hindus say they are the seven rishis or gods, attendant

[4] According to some writers, Uranus at least may have been known to the ancients, although rediscovered in modern times.

upon the Supreme Deity. In China they were supposed to form the celestial Government.

It may be of interest to give the Arabic names and identify with the Hindu rishis, as in the following table:

| Greek Letter | Arabic Name | Hindu Rishi |
|---|---|---|
| Alpha | Dubhe | Kratu |
| Beta | Mirak | Pulaha |
| Gamma | Phacd | Pulastya |
| Delta | Megrez | Atri |
| Epsilon | Alioth | Angiras |
| Zeta | Mizar | Vashishtha |
| Eta | Benatnasch | Marichi |

The idea of higher octaves is of some interest as showing the ancients had some conception of a galaxy beyond the solar system, and a universe beyond the galaxy.

## The Seven Gods

The modern English names of the planets are taken from Roman mythology, except that we use the Anglo-Saxon for Sol the sun-god and Luna the moon god. The sun's symbol is ⊙ and the moon's ☽. Mercury, known as Hermes by the Greeks, was the messenger of the gods, patron of travellers and conductor of the souls of the dead. He is represented as a young man with a *petasus* or winged cap, wings for his feet called *talaria* and a short sword called *herpe* and a wand the *caduceus*. His symbol ☿ is supposed to represent the last named. Venus was goddess of love and beauty, represented as a beautiful girl, scantily clothed, wearing a *cestus* or girdle and carrying a mirror which is represented by her symbol ♀. She was called Aphrodite by the Greeks. Mars was god of war, and he is represented as armed, with shield and spear, which together make up his symbol ♂. He was known as Ares by the Greeks. Jupiter, the Greek Zeus, king of the gods, is represented as a bearded man, sitting on a throne of gold and ivory,

carrying the thunderbolt, represented by his symbol ♃.
Saturn, known to the Greeks as Cronus, god of time, was
represented as an old man with a scythe and hour-glass. The
scythe is represented by his symbol ♄.

Sol or the Sun (Helios of the Greeks) was often replaced
by Apollo or Phoebus, god of medicine and the arts. Likewise
Luna or the Moon (Selene of the Greeks) was replaced by
Diana, goddess of hunting.

The seven gods are easily distinguishable in the mythology
of most religions. Among the Hindus there were special gods
for the planets; these were apparently only special forms of
the better known gods or goddesses. The planets are all regarded as male[5] by the Hindus, but they are assigned to the
same days of the week as in the West. The Sun is Ravi, a form
of the sun-god Surya, an important deity in the Vedas. His
daily journey through the sky, like the Greek Helios, is accom-
plished in a chariot, in this case drawn by seven horses, pre-
ceded, as in the Greek story, by the goddess of the dawn.
Chandra is the moon, also called Soma, a name also applied
to the elixir of the gods.[6] Budha is the planet Mercury, not
to be confused with Gautama Buddha, the ninth incarnation
of Vishnu, Sukra is the planet Venus, Angaraka or Mangala
is the planet Mars and god of war, Guru or Brihaspati is the
planet Jupiter and symbolic of the priesthood, Sani is the
planet Saturn, called the slow-moving one.

In ancient Egypt the sun-god was Ra. He travelled through
the sky in a boat. Khons or Khensu, the moon, was represented
by a male, shown with the head of a hawk, surmounted by
the moon's disc. Thoth, guide of the dead, was obviously
Mercury. He was represented with the head of an ibis. Hathor,
goddess of love and beauty corresponds with Venus. She is

---

[5] But in astrology, according to B. V. Ramann, noted Indian
astrologer (*A Manual of Hindu Astrology,* Bangalore, not dated)
it is admitted that the moon and Venus are treated as females.

[6] See W. B. Crow : *The Occult Properties of Herbs,* London,
1969.

sometimes represented as a cow, or with the head of a cow, at other times as a beautiful girl. Menthu, Munt or Mont was the falcon-headed war god, probably the equivalent of Mars. Amen, Ammon or Amun, sometimes given the head of a ram, was the undoubted equivalent of Jupiter. Geb, an earth god is the Egyptian Saturn (*i*) because he seized power from his father, as Saturn did from Uranus, (*ii*) because, as an earth god, he presided over agriculture, as did Saturn. He is represented with a goose on his head.

The Babylonian mythology also shows the seven planetary gods quite plainly. Shamash was the sun-god, with the usual daily journey across the sky. Sin was the moon-god, with a corresponding nightly journey. Nabu corresponds with Mercury, being the messenger and scribe of the gods. Ishtar corresponds with Venus, having several myths in common with the latter, *e.g.* her love for Tammuz, corresponding with that of Venus for Adonis. Ninib corresponds with Mars, being the god of death and war. Marduk was the chief of the gods and corresponds with Jupiter. The Phoenician El corresponds with Cronus, having dethroned his father Uranus, a well known story in Greek mythology. He was Hasis-Atra of Semitic mythology. The Phoenician, Syrian and primtive Arabic gods were the same as the Babylonian except in name, and several appear in Hebrew form in the Old Testament.

In Moslem legends we encounter the names of the planets, although, of course, they are not worshipped. The Arabic names are : ☉ Shams, ☽ Qamar, ☿ Utarid, ♀ Zurah, ♂ Mirrikh, ♃ Mushtari, ♄ Zuhal. The Persian names are : ☉ Kurshad, ☽ Mah, ☿ Zir, ♀ Nahid, ♂ Bahram, ♃ Harmuzd, ♄ Kanian.

The Zoroastrians believe in six holy immortal spirits ministering to the Supreme Being, and also in one powerful evil being. The good spirits were called *Amshaspands* or *Amesha Spentas* and are as follows : (*i*) Vohu Manah or Bahman, symbolizing good thought and acting as protector of animal life: (*ii*) Khshatra Vairya or Sharevah representing good government and protector of metals; (*iii*) Asha Vahishta or Ardabahisht, symbolizing good virtue and controlling fire; (*iv*) Spenta Armaiti or Asfandarmad, representing good harmony and controlling earth; (*v*) Ameretat or Murdad meaning immortality and protecting plant life; and (*vi*) Haurvatat or Khurdad, symbolizing good health and protector of the element water.

The evil principle is Ahriman or Angra Mainyu, the opponent of the good god Ormuzd or Ahura Mazda. Zoroastrianism, however, is not a dualistic religion, for Ahriman is limited in his power and will be overthrown at the end of the world.

In several other mythologies we encounter the set of seven. In British legend, for instance, the famous king Bran invades Ireland. He is killed and only seven survivors return to Great Britain. They include the famous bard Taliesin and they have some very strange adventures.

In Slavonic mythology there were supposed to be seven winds and seven planets.

Even among the natives of America we find the seven. For instance, among the Aztecs of Mexico we find references to the Seven Caverns of Refuge from the Flood and the Seven Cities of Origin.

In the Taoist religion of China there are seven planetary beasts: Unicorn (♄), panther (♃), bear (♂), lion (☉), seal (♀), rhinoceros (☿) and sea-horse (☽). They also had a series of birds, as follows: pelican (♄), peacock (♃), white pheasant (♂), sun-crow or golden hen (☉), quail (♀), mandarin duck (☿), and long-tailed jay (☽).

In the Lamaist religion of Tibet there were seven Heroic Buddhas or Tathagatas. They were Vipasyin (♄), Sikhin (♃), Visvabhu (♂), Krakucandra (☉), Kanaka-muni (♀), Kasyapa (☿) and Sakya-Muni, the historical Buddha (☽). They also had seven medical buddhas and seven precious things, etc.

The seven gods of luck of the Japanese are well known as

they are frequently figured. Ebisu, the god of work, is shown as a fisherman. Daikoku, the god of wealth, is shown with a hammer and bags of rice. Benzaiten is the goddess of love and rides on a dragon or snake. Bishamonten is god of victory. He holds a lance and a miniature pagoda. Fukurokuju is god of longevity and is represented with a very tall skull; he is accompanied by a bird of the stork species. Jurojin is god of luck, holds a staff and is accompanied by an animal of the stag species. Hotei-osho is god of contentment and is represented with a screen and a sac and is always shown as a fat man with a shaven head. Three of these gods[7] are always shown with much enlarged ear lobes, a feature which connects them with the mysterious inhabitants of Easter Island.

## Seven in the Apocalypse

In the last book of the New Testament, the *Apocalypse* of St. John, there are references to seven stars and seven golden candlesticks (*Apoc* ii, 1). They are the seven spirits before the throne of God (*Apoc* i, 4, iii, 1, iv, 5). They are also characterized as seven eyes, which are the seven spirits of God (*Apoc* v, 6). They are mentioned in the Old Testament in the book of *Zacharias* or *Zechariah* iv, 2. The seven spirits were formerly reverenced in the Catholic Church and the number seven has an important part to play in Christian symbolism.[8]

Michael (meaning 'like unto God') is described as a chief or great prince (*Dan* x, 13, 21, xii, 1) and disputes with the devil over the body of Moses (*Jude* 9) and is well known as the leader in casting down the devil (described as a dragon) with his angels (*Apoc* xii, 7). He probably corresponds with

[7] The first two and last named.

[8] See W. B. Crow : Astronomical Religion, *Mysteries of the Ancients* No. 6, London, 1942. For further allusions to the number seven see H. Grattan Guiness : *Creation centred in Christ,* London, 1896 and E. W. Bullinger, *Number in Scripture,* 3rd ed., London, 1913.

Mercury, as the slayer of the hundred-eyed Argus. He is also identified with the constellation Hercules, who is shown in the celestial globe as slaying the dragon Python.

Gabriel (meaning 'strength of god') appears in *Daniel* viii, 16 and ix, 21 as an interpreter and in *Luke* i, 26 at the Annunciation, also in *Luke* i, 11 in the announcement of the forthcoming birth of St. John the Baptist. He is alleged by Moslems to have revealed the *Koran* to Mohammed. He is connected with the moon and with the constellation Aquila.

Raphael (meaning 'divine virtue') appears in *Tobit* xii, 15 and the whole book concerns one of his beneficent ministrations. He is a healer and is represented by the sun. He is also the constellation Ophiuchus, a man wrestling with the serpent of disease.

Uriel (meaning fire or light of God) appears in what is often called the *Second Book of Esdras*[9] where he enlightens the prophet. He is also said to have befriended Adam and Eve and afterwards Seth and Enoch and to have protected the sepulchre of our Lord. He may be identical with Chamuel or Chamael identified with the planet Mars and the constellation of Lupus the wolf.

Anael (meaning 'hear us, O Lord') is little known but appears to correspond with the planet Venus and the small constellation of *Asellus*, the asses, being also related to *Taurus*, the bull.

Zadkiel (meaning righteousness of God) was said to have been the angel who prevented Abraham's sacrifice of his son. He corresponds with the planet Jupiter and the constellation *Ursa Major*, the great bear.

Cassiel (meaning throne of God), who was said to have acted as a guide to the Jews in the wilderness, corresponds with the planet Saturn and the constellation of *Capricorn*, the goat.

---

[9] More correctly the *fourth*, as the second is a synonym for that of *Nehemiah*.

## The Seven Heavens

The phrase *the seven heavens* is often used, but is not strictly in accord with sacred tradition, since (*i*) some of the seven appear to have been divided and (*ii*) there were more than seven, although it was usual to ascribe seven to the planets. This, at any rate, applies to the Christian system.

The Mohammedan system seems to have been less complex. The prophet is said,[10] during the Night-Journey, to have passed through seven heavens, as follows[11] : (*i*) the heaven of silver, corresponding with the moon, wherein were Adam and Eve; (*ii*) of white gold, corresponding with Mercury, wherein was Enoch; (*iii*) of copper, corresponding with Venus, wherein was Aaron; (*iv*) of gold, corresponding with the sun, wherein were Jesus and John the Baptist; (*v*) of steel, corresponding with Mars, wherein was Noah, (*vi*) of precious stones, corresponding with Jupiter, wherein was Moses; (*vii*) of light, corresponding with Saturn, wherein was Abraham.

## Hell, Purgatory and Paradise

The Christian scheme may be illustrated from Dante (1265–1321) who in his most important work (*The Divine Comedy*) gives the late mediaeval conceptions of the after life. It is in three parts. The first part deals with Hell or the Infernal Regions, (*Inferno*). This includes Limbo, divided into parts, then seven circles and finally a pit called Malêbolgê for the devil and fallen angels, who are identified with the giants who rebelled against Jupiter. On leaving the infernal region Dante enters *Purgatory*, at the gate of which a porter marks him with seven marks, representing sins, telling him he will lose one at each stage, in consonance with the idea that Purgatory is the place of purification. Finally Dante enters Heaven (*Paradise*), which consists of ten spheres. From below upwards

[10] In the traditions *Mishkat* xxiv, 7.
[11] The translations and planetary ascriptions are very uncertain.

these are as follows: (*i*) The lowermost is the sphere of the moon and this is inhabited by angels; (*ii*) the next is that of Mercury, where dwell the archangels; (*iii*) the third is of Venus, wherein are the spirits called virtues; (*iv*) the fourth of the sun, wherein are the powers; (*v*) the fifth of Mars, wherein are the principalities; (*vi*) the sixth of Jupiter, wherein are dominions or dominations; (*vii*) the seventh of Saturn, wherein are spirits called thrones. Beyond these are (*viii*) the eighth sphere, that of the fixed stars, wherein dwell the cherubim; then comes (*ix*) the ninth sphere, which is that of the *primum mobile*, the sphere within which all heavenly bodies revolve containing the seraphim; finally there is (*x*) the last or tenth sphere, the *Empyrean* or *Empyreum*, the sphere of unbodied light, the home of the Virgin Mary and the Holy Trinity. The various lower spheres are also the abode of many who have been saints on earth. For instance, St. Francis and St. Augustine were seen in the third sphere of heaven.

It is clear that the ten heavens of mediaeval Christianity embody the idea of the nine hierarchies of St. Dionysius the Areopagite and the ten sephiroth of the qabalists.

In India the seven heavens were situated on the fabulous Mount Meru and were the homes of the various gods. Originally it was a Vedic concept, but it was accepted by later Hinduism and by Buddhism. It was supposed to be situated at the centre of the earth, and was apparently believed by some to be an actual mountain, to the north of the Himalayas. At its top was Brahmapura, the residence of Brahma. Nearby was Vaikuntha the home of Vishnu and Kailasa where dwell Siva, Kubera and Ganesha. Indra's abode was Swarga, a portion of Mount Meru, where dwell many inferior gods and saints, and so on. Below Mount Meru is Patala, the Hindu infernal regions where dwell the Nagas or serpent gods. This is also divided into seven and in the lowest realm, Vasaki, the great earth serpent rules, just as Satan dominates the lowest realm of the Christian hell.

The Greeks seem to have adopted the idea of Mount Meru,

as their home of the gods is a very similar mount, called Olympus. It is usually thought to have been north of Greece proper, in Macedonia or Thrace.

## Seven in Philosophy

In Hindu philosophy, which is accepted by many of the Buddhists too, the Universe is divided into seven planes. Each of these is further subdivided, in theory into seven subdivisions, in practice a lesser number serve ordinary purposes.

A plane is regarded as a manifestation of some aspect of the Cosmic Existence of the One Divine Existence. The higher planes seem to be aspects of what we call the transcendence of the Godhead, the lower of His immanence. At the same time, it appears, the higher planes represent the subjective worlds, the lower the objective. The higher planes tend to be regarded as more real than the lower, which are the worlds of *Maya*, that is to say, illusion.

However we must outline, briefly, the nature of these seven planes. They are as follows:

(*i*) *Sthûla* the physical plane, *i.e.* what Western physical science calls matter and energy, which materialism regards as the sole reality; in it human beings manifest as the physical body (*sthûla-sharîra* or *anna-mayâ-kosha*);

(*ii*) *Kâma*, the plane of feelings, desires and passions, the world of emotion, manifesting in the human being as what Paracelsus called *the sidereal body*, which afterwards came to be known as *the astral body* (*kâma-rûpa*). Kâma or the astral world was so called because, to clairvoyant vision, objects appeared shining against a dark background, like stars in a night sky;

(*iii*) *Manas*, the plane of thought, ideas and intelligence, the mental world, manifesting in man as the mental body, (*manasa-rupa*);

(*iv*) *Buddhi*, commonly called the plane of intuition in the

West, where the latter refers, in its strictly philosophical sense to a direct apprehension of consciousness, including the reality of universals, of values and eternal truths. In man it manifests, usually only feebly, as what is called the body of bliss;

(v) *Atma* a still higher world where the divine occasionally breaks through or manifests in this imperfect world, as in Christian theology the Holy Ghost inspires, even if faintly on most occasions, all truly spiritual activities or as in the partial avatars of Krishna in Hinduism. It is sometimes called the Nirvanic plane;

(vi) *Anupadaka* a still higher plane, where the divine life manifests in the perfect, as in the life of Christ, in Christianity or the full avatar of Vishnu, namely Krishna, in Hinduism;

(vii) *Adi* the highest plane of all, God the Father in Christianity or Brahma in Hinduism.

Thus the Universe consists of seven worlds, interpenetrating one another, according to this oriental philosophy, adopted in the Western world by the theosophists. Perhaps a rough analogy might be that the higher penetrates the lower, much in the same way that a dissolved substance penetrates the liquid wherein it is dissolved. Something of the sort is implied in the New Testament where Jesus speaks of salt which has lost its savour (*Matt* v, 13; *Mark* ix, 49; *Luke* xiv, 34).

The Hindu system includes all the senses in the physical world and the forces observed by them constitute the physical aspect of *Fohat*, which is said to have seven sons, being the various forms of physical energy, such as heat, light and sound, electricity and magnetism, chemical energy and mechanical energy, amongst those recognized in the science of physics.

## Kundalini

But besides Fohat there is another force, unknown to the physicists, called *Kundalini*. This is a latent power in the human body which can be aroused by certain yogic practices.

When so activated it sets in motion seven chief[12] centres in the astral body, and harmonizes them with striking results for the powers latent in man. These centres are called *chakras*. They are supposed to have been seen by clairvoyants, who have given the following descriptions. Each is represented in the physical body by a nerve centre. They are said to exist on all planes, so it is not unexpected that they are said to be represented in ordinary gross anatomy, although only by nerve centres. The clairvoyant gives a very different account of them, showing lotus-like forms of bright colours.

In the human being who has not cultivated Yoga, kundalini is pictured as a coiled up serpent, lying around or near the lowermost chakra. As the yogi progresses in his training, kundalini uncoils and rises through the various chakras, and as it does so the yogi obtains various powers.

The *muladhara chakra* lies in front of the lower part of the sacrum. It is described as crimson in colour,[13] with four petals. By activating this chakra the yogi is said[14] to obtain (*i*) freedom from disease, (*ii*) knowledge of past and future, (*iii*) psychic powers. Rele[15] identifies it with the pelvic plexus.

The *swâdhisthâna chakra* lies in the pelvic cavity, just above the preceding. This has six petals and its colour is described as vermilion. By its contemplation, it is said, freedom from disease is obtained, and death is warded off. Rele[16] thinks it probably is the hypogastric plexus, or sex centre.

The *manipura plexus* is found on the level of the umbilicus, just below the diaphragm, at the back of the abdominal cavity. It is of a brilliant golden colour, it is connected with

---

[12] There are really a considerable number of chakras, just as there are many planets. But symbolism of the seven great centres corresponds with the seven planets of astrology, not of astronomy.

[13] J. Marquès-Rivière : *Tantric Yoga, Hindu and Tibetan,* (trans.), London, not dated, from authentic Eastern manuscripts.

[14] Vasant G. Rele : *The Mysterious Kundalini,* 3rd ed., Bombay, 1931.

[15] *loc. cit.*

[16] *loc. cit.*

gold and the sun, and has been called *the city of gems*. It has ten petals. When the Kundalini reaches and activates it, the yogi is said to be able to discover medicines and hidden treasures. It is represented in the physical body by the epigastric or coeliac plexus, formerly called the solar plexus from its radiating appearance.

The *anahata chakra* surrounds the heart. It is described as yellow or as blood-red, with twelve petals. It is said to be the seat of *prana* or vitality. When the kundalini invests it, the yogi can acquire clairvoyance, clairaudience and ability to travel at will through space. It obviously corresponds with the cardiac plexus, or plexus of the heart in the physical body.

The *vishudda chakra* or throat centre lies near the larynx. It is golden with sixteen petals. By means of this lotus the yogi is further purified, and is said to be made capable of living youthfully for a thousand years. Rele thinks it may be identified with the pharyngeal plexus in the physical body.

The *taluka chakra* is situated on a level of the base of the nose, between the eyes. It is like a bright light when activated and is called the *third eye*. It has two petals. On reaching this, the kundalini confers on the yogi very high powers over the universe. In the physical body it corresponds with the cavernous plexus.

The *brahmarandhra chakra* is situated at the top of the head. It is white in colour and has a thousand petals. When Kundalini reaches this the yogi has acquired his highest powers. In the physical body it corresponds with the brain or part thereof.

How do the seven chakras correspond with the seven planets? Judging from the rulership of the organs of the body commonly accepted, the brain centre is ruled by the moon and the heart centre by the sun. The throat centre pertains to Venus, as this planet is said to rule the larynx, an organ which projects from the front of the neck where it forms an elevation[17] called Adam's apple, and the apple is well known

[17] More prominent in the male, however.

as the fruit of Venus. Hence the popular association of the fruit given to Adam by Eve in the Garden of Eden which resulted in the Fall. If these planetary assignments are correct then it is very likely that the rise of Kundalini is in line with the order of the planets as given by the rapidity of movement, beginning with the slowest, thus:

(*i*) *muladhara* corresponding with Saturn;
(*ii*) *swâdhisthâna* corresponding with Jupiter;
(*iii*) *manipura* corresponding with Mars;
(*iv*) *anahata* corresponding with the Sun;
(*v*) *vishudda* corresponding with Venus;
(*vi*) *taluka* corresponding with Mercury;
(*vii*) *brahmarandhra* corresponding with the Moon.

## Stages of Human Life

Most people are familiar with Shakespeare's idea of the seven ages of man in his play *As you like it*. The stages are represented as the infant, the schoolboy, the lover, the soldier, the justice, the pantaloon and finally extreme senility. This is somewhat crude, but may represent some old tradition of seven ages of post-natal life.

Some say that the human body changes every seven years. The change of teeth is practically completed at the age of seven, puberty sets in at fourteen, the skeleton is completed at the age of twenty-one. In the female the menopause, in healthy individuals, should take place around the age of forty-nine, although, owing to unnatural conditions it often occurs earlier. There is the *great climacteric* for both sexes around sixty-three, and we are told by a practitioner that seven years earlier, at fifty-six, there is often a critical year. Seventy ('three score years and ten') is also a dangerous year and is popularly supposed to mark the end of life (although there are records of individuals having lived twice this age!)

Can modern science discover anything like the seven ages

of man? The Freudian school of psychanalysts distinguish (*i*) an *early oral* stage in the first year when there is no object love and the psychic energy (the libido) is centred in the mouth, (*ii*) a *late oral* stage (after weaning in most European countries) when the teeth are beginning and biting occurs, (*iii*) an *early anal* stage and (*iv*) a *late anal* stage, the last two occurring in the second and third year, (*v*) a *phallic* period when libido begins to invest the organs of sex, it is said to begin at the fourth year, but the sex organs are by no means fully developed and it passes over to a latent period, during which they remain inactive. Finally, (*vi*) at the age of puberty the sex organs become fully developed, can function normally and reproduction can occur. This is called the *genital* phase. If we add (*vii*) a *post-genital*, after the menopause in women and after the grand climacteric in men we can reckon seven stages from birth onward.

However we ought perhaps to count two stages before birth. We can then count seven still more fundamental stages:

(*i*) From conception to the completion of the placenta, the offspring being only an *embryo* which can be seen to belong to the vertebrate group. This extends in the human subject no longer than the first two months.

(*ii*) From placenta-formation to birth, the offspring being now called a *foetus* which means that it can be identified as a placental mammal; at this stage muscular movements are shown; they become perceptible at what is called *quickening* which is well marked at sixteen weeks.

Birth normally occurs at the end of the ninth calendar month. According to the psychologist O. Rank,[18] birth has a profound influence for later life since it gives the individual a sort of shock, which he calls the *trauma of birth* producing a primal anxiety of separation, which is revived later at weaning, at imagined threats of castration and all kinds of separations. Religion, according to Rank, is an organized attempt

[18] O. Rank: *The Trauma of Birth*, trans., New York, 1929.

to re-establish the intra-uterine condition. The temple, therefore, is a maternal body. Not only is the house one of the symbols of the body in dream analysis, but in the physical place of worship the sanctuary, choir and nave represent head, thorax and abdomen.[19] Further, the human body represents the cosmos, which explains the *melothesia* or zodiacal diagrams which were representations of the body inscribed with the symbols of the planets and signs of the zodiac on various parts.

(*iii*) From birth to the period of standing erect, called the *oral* stage by Freud, which is the suckling period of Western peoples[20] and lasts about one year. Speech may begin at the end of this period, but of course this varies very much in development and is a gradual acquisition.

(*iv*) From the period of standing erect to the period of becoming a self-conscious individual. Consciousness of individuality is said to set in when the child uses the personal pronoun I. Before this the child refers to himself in the third person. After this, writing begins to be learnt. Freud calls this the *anal* stage and believes it generally lasts through the second and third year.

(*v*) From the period of self-consciousness to the time of puberty, called by Freud the *phallic* or *Oedipal* period. This begins in the fourth year, but passes over into a *latent period* (from lack of emotional change) until puberty, when the conflict about the *Oedipus complex* revives.[21]

(*vi*) From puberty to menopause in the female (thirteen to forty-nine) or to the grand climacteric in the male (fourteen to sixty-three) during which the genitals can function normally

[19] W. B. Crow : Human Anatomy in Temple Architecture. *Mysteries of the Ancients*, 4, London, 1942. This work explains the idea in much greater detail.

[20] Suckling is much extended in Japan, but this is probably artificial and is believed to be contraceptive.

[21] For explanation of the various terms related to psychoanalysis, see the works of Freud and his followers.

and reproduction can occur, but very variable. This phase is called the *genital phase*.

(*vii*) After the menopause in women and the grand climacteric in men, the genitals can still function normally, but reproduction is almost impossible in women and is somewhat unlikely in men. *Senescence* is common in this phase but sometimes occurs earlier.

## Seven in History

To some extent the life of man repeats the history of the World, or even of the Universe. The intra-uterine condition, the life in the womb before birth, is characterized by depth-psychologists as one in which all wants are satisfied. It is a repetition of the Golden Age or Paradise. The Fall of Man is repeated when birth occurs. Paradise, from the biological point of view, is life in the sea. There are myths and fairy-tales which picture a life of bliss in a realm under the sea, as in Keltic legends, Japanese fairy tales and the Arabian nights stories. According to biology primitive life was in the sea, and only later emerged on the land. The life cycle of an amphibian, like a frog or newt, is an intermediate stage, the tadpole being aquatic, the adult a land animal. Birth represents, and in embryology corresponds with, emergence from the water, for life in the womb is actually aquatic and only after birth is the young baby compelled to use lungs to breathe air.

Theosophists have a scheme[22] wherein mankind is thought to inhabit seven planets in succession and on this earth to manifest as seven root races on seven different continents. It is derived from Hindu mythology. In the *Puranas* the seven continents are named (*i*) Jambu, (*ii*) Plaksha, (*iii*) Shalmali, (*iv*) Kusha, (v) Kraunca, (*vi*) Shaka and (*vii*) Pushkara. The inhabitants of the last two have not yet materialized. The fifth

[22] A. E. Powell : *The Solar System*, London, 1930, gives full details of the somewhat complex history.

is represented by what anthropologists call the Caucasians, *viz.* the majority of Europeans, Persians, Indians, Arabs and Jews. The fourth includes the Mongolian races, *viz.* Chinese, Japanese, Siamese, Redskins, etc. which probably form the majority group in the world today, but which are supposed to be direct descendants of the inhabitants of Atlantis. The latter, as described by Plato, lived in the great continent in the Atlantic Ocean and spread east and west. This continent of Atlantis was submerged in the Biblical Flood. Stories of the catastrophe are recorded in mythology all over the world.[23] There is much nonsense written about this, but adverse critics of the historical truth of these legends seem to be completely ignorant of the vast amount of strictly scientific evidence.[24] The third of the lost continents corresponds with the continent of Lemuria, between Africa and the East Indies, the inhabitants of which may still be represented by the Australian aborigines and to some extent by the Negroes. Some wild fantasies have also been written about Lemuria but equally there are definite evidences.[25] The first and second root races, according to the theosophists, were immaterial, so remains of these are not expected. On the other hand, the second continent has been identified with the mythical Hyperborea, and evidence has been given that there were inhabitants of both the sub-arctic and even arctic regions.[26]

[23] W. B. Crow : Noah's Ark, *Mysteries of the Ancients,* 5, London, 1942.
[24] Lewis Spence : *The History of Atlantis,* London, not dated, and *The Problem of Atlantis,* London, 1924, revised edition, 1925, may be cited as strictly scientific for the most part. The author was recognized as a learned archaeologist before he began his researches on Atlantis and Lemuria.
[25] Lewis Spence : *The Problem of Lemuria,* 2nd impression, London, 1933, is one of the best books on this subject.
[26] L. B. G. Tilak : *The Arctic Home in the Vedas,* Poona, 1903, reprinted 1925, 1956.

## Seven in Nature

Ignoring several arbitrary lists of seven, such as the seven sleepers, the seven champions of Christendom and the seven wonders of the world, we do find some natural scales of seven, like the seven notes of the diatonic scale in music, the seven basic vowels in phonology and the seven colours of the spectrum in optics.

CHAPTER VI

# *The Zodiac*

## The Twelve Signs

The word *zodiac* means the circle of the beasts. All the signs are called after human figures or those of some animal, the balance *Libra* excepted.[1] The twelve zodiacal signs are not to be confused with the twelve constellations which form a zone around the middle of the celestial sphere, although named after them in classical times. The zodiac is older than the constellations, most of which have names derived from Roman mythology. The zodiac is divided into twelve sections (the signs) of equal parts of thirty degrees each. The constellations were of somewhat varying size. The zodiac, as a whole, moves through the constellations. Although some of the uninitiated Roman writers may have confused the two systems, the difference was known to the Greeks. It is from Plato we have the idea of the Platonic year and month. The zodiac is measured from the equinox and solstices, and the Platonic year is the time taken by any of these points to have moved through the circle of the constellations. This cosmic period lasted about 26,000 years. Each Platonic month is reckoned about 2,160 years and is supposed to be a period of distinctive culture. We are now nearing the end of the Era of Pisces, because the Vernal Equinox, which is counted as

[1] This may explain the curious fact that for a time among the Greeks and Romans only eleven zodiacal constellations were named, Libra being represented as the claws of the scorpion. However this was only a phase among the uninitiated; the twelve gods of the zodiacal signs and constellations being well known in the early history of Egypt.

the beginning of the zodiac, is about to leave that constellation.

Although each sign of the zodiac has its own peculiar influence,[2] nevertheless each sign is *ruled* by a particular planet, which is particularly congenial to that sign. The same planet in the opposite sign is said to be in *detriment*, and fails to show its power. Each planet is said to *exalted* in a particular sign, wherein it shows its best feature and to have its *fall* in the opposite sign, wherein it shows its worst. Signs are divided into cardinal, fixed and common,[3] also into fiery, airy, watery and earthy, according to the four elements with which they are connected. Many other features of signs are described in books on astrology, but we must make some remarks about them here as they are among the best of all symbols, being almost universally applicable.

Aries is a cardinal fiery sign represented by a ram. Its ruler is Mars and the Sun is exalted therein. It rules the head, including the face. It signifies energy. Among the Romans Aries was assigned to the goddess Minerva, who was fabled to have arisen fully armed from the head of Jupiter, the king of the gods. Minerva was the virgin goddess of war and all the arts and crafts.

Taurus is a fixed earthy sign represented by a bull. The ruler is the planet Venus and the Moon was exalted therein. Taurus rules the neck, the throat and the larynx. It signifies inertia and fertility. Venus among the Romans was the goddess ascribed to Taurus.

Gemini is a common airy sign. Its symbol is the twins, said to be Castor and Pollux, whose myth refers to the alternation of light and darkness. Gemini rules the lungs and the respiratory tract. Although Mercury rules this sign the Roman god

[2] It must not be supposed that the author is giving any credit to the idea of predetermined fate. In the normal human subject influences are subject to the free-will of the individual.

[3] Cardinal refers to the quality of *rajas* in Hinduism, referring to activity, fixed to *tamas* or inertia and common to *sattva* or rhythm.

ascribed to Gemini was Apollo. It signifies speech and logical thought.

Cancer is a cardinal watery sign, its symbol being the crab. The Moon rules this sign and Jupiter is exalted therein. In the human body Cancer rules the breasts and internally the stomach. In the psyche it refers to emotion, especially the maternal feelings. Among the Romans the god assigned to Cancer was Mercury.

Leo is a fixed fiery sign, represented by the Lion. The Sun is the ruler. Leo rules the heart, the blood circulation and the dorsal surface or back of the body. In the psyche it refers to the ego and individuality. The Romans assigned Jupiter to this sign, in spite of the solar rulership, as he was their king of the gods.

Virgo is a common earthy sign. Its symbol is a virgin carrying an ear of corn. Both the rulership and the exaltation are taken to be Mercury. Virgo rules the intestines in the human body and in the psyche refers to discrimination. The Romans assigned to Virgo the goddess of corn, Ceres.

Libra is a cardinal airy sign. Its symbol is the balance. It is ruled by Venus. In this sign Saturn is exalted. Libra rules the kidneys which is appropriate enough, as this seventh sign is concerned with equilibrium both in body and mind. As the realm of Libra covers the fine arts the Roman fabled that it was to be assigned to Vulcan, god of arts and crafts, husband of Venus.

Scorpio is a fixed watery sign, symbolized by the scorpion. It rules the genital organs and the sex instinct. The planet Mars is the ruler and the god Mars was assigned by the Romans.

Sagittarius is a common fiery sign, symbolized by a centaur shooting an arrow. Jupiter is said to be the ruler. In the body it is supposed to control the muscles, the hips and thighs. The Romans assigned the virgin goddess of hunting, Diana, to Sagittarius.

Capricorn is a cardinal earthy sign. Its symbol is a goat. It is ruled by Saturn, and Mars is in exaltation in this sign. It rules the bones and the knees. In the psyche it refers to efforts and endeavour. The goddess of the hearth, Vesta, was assigned to Capricorn by the Romans.

Aquarius is a fixed airy sign. Its symbol is the water pourer, a figure pouring out water, as rain from the air. This sign is ruled by Saturn. It seems to rule the skin,[4] but is generally assigned to the ankles. Psychologically it refers to science and technology. The queen of the gods, Juno, was ascribed to Aquarius by the Romans, but it had some connections both with Ganymede and Uranus.

Pisces is a common watery sign. Its symbol was two fish, joined together by a band. Jupiter is the ruler and Venus is exalted in this sign. It rules the lymphatic system and the feet[5] in the human body, and poetry and imagination in the psyche. The Romans said it belonged to the god of the sea, Neptune.

## Zodiacal Gods

All over the world each national culture has its favourite gods, but these are not chosen by chance, or in an arbitrary fashion. Their deities form a hierarchy, an organized structure, wherein each god or goddess occupies a particular place. We have already seen that there are, in many religions, three supreme gods, four or five gods of the elements and seven

[4] W. B. Crow: Animals of the Zodiac, *Astrology: the Astrologers' Quarterly* VI, 4, 1933, page 215.

[5] If Pisces rules the feet, Aquarius the ankles and Capricorn the knees then Virgo, Leo and Cancer the opposite signs should rule hands, wrist and elbow. The hands are certainly related to Virgo, the neat and tidy sign, the wrists display the circulatory system in the pulse and the elbows and forearms are prominent in the crab. This was pointed out by the present author, in lectures and writings (The Human Body as a Solar System, *Occult Review*, Oct. and Nov., 1932, reprinted in *Mysteries of the Ancients*, 18, 1945) many years ago.

planetary rulers. Now we have to add the twelve gods of the zodiac.

The Romans had the twelve Consentes or *dii consulentes, viz.* the twelve major gods already mentioned in describing the zodiacal signs. The Greeks had the same twelve, using the names Athena, Aphrodite, Phoebus, Hermes, Zeus, Demeter, Hephaestus, Ares, Artermis, Hestia, Hera and Poseidon, in the order given. The Greeks had an earlier twelve of titans, who were displaced later by the major gods. The latter were sometimes denominated Olympians, from their inhabiting Mount Olympus.

Herodotus, in his well known *History*, says the Greek gods were, with few exceptions, obtained from the ancient Egyptians. Some of the aforementioned can be identified with their deities, *e.g.* Neith is the prototype of Athena, Hathor of Aphrodite, Thoth of Hermes, Ammon of Zeus, etc. Athena was also known among the Cretans and Etruscans. Hera, who was not represented among the Egyptian goddesses, was known in Crete and Poseidon in Libya and Crete. The twelve gods and goddesses were probably known in Babylon and Phoenicia. Among the Zoroastrians of ancient Persia their place was taken by the spiritual beings called Yazatas which correspond with the zodiacal constellations. Among the Hindus there are the twelve Adityas. Among the Norsemen the Aesir represent the twelve chief gods and there was a somewhat less important group of twelve, the Vanir.

The Slavs have their twelve kingdoms of the sun, the Taoists have their twelve ornaments, the Japanese refer to twelve sacred cushions on which the Deity is enthroned. The ornaments of the Taoists in general have an individual connection with the twelve signs, thus (*i*) flames representing Aries, a fiery sign, sun exalted; (*ii*) sprays of an aquatic grass, vegetation being harmonious to Taurus, and dampness suggesting the moon which is exalted in this sign; (*iii*) two pheasants for Gemini, the pair suggesting twins, and birds are ruled by this sign; (*iv*) the moon with a frog, indicative of Cancer, a watery sign, ruled by the moon; (*v*) the sun with a three-legged red crow, a sign of the sun which rules Leo; (*vi*) millet grains, suggesting Virgo, sometimes represented in the West merely by an ear of wheat; (*vii*) vessels used in the rituals of the temple, which are quite appropriate to Libra; (*viii*) a sort of weapon, obviously suitable for Scorpio, ruled by Mars, god of war; (*ix*) stars arranged in a pattern, as in a constellation with connecting lines, the connection with Sagittarius being less easy to trace; (*x*) mountains representing Capricorn, the sign of the mountain climber; (*xi*) a bat, an animal regarded as lucky by the Chinese, representing Aquarius for no very obvious reason; (*xii*) a pair of five-clawed dragons taking the place of the pair of fishes representing Pisces in the West.

## The Twelve Apostles

The twelve first chosen by Christ were supposed to be drawn from the twelve tribes of the *Old Testament*, one from each tribe. Furthermore, each tribe had its correspondence with one of the twelve precious stones on the breastplate of the High Priest, and each of these also corresponded with one sign of the zodiac. Authors are not all agreed on the correspondences of apostles, tribes, precious stones and the signs of the zodiac, but we have given some indications in an earlier work.[6]

The twelve apostles occupy a place in the Church which corresponds with the place of the zodiacal signs in the heavens. Another tradition avers that the Creed, which was formerly called the Symbol, consisted of twelve articles, each of which was contributed by one of the Apostles.

In the *Old Testament* there are twelve patriarchs from Sem (Shem) to Jacob and the twelve sons of the last names formed the original twelve tribes. Some other names were included, with corresponding omissions but there are always twelve. Even in the *Apocalypse* there are the same number. Going

[6] W. B. Crow: *Precious Stones, their occult power and hidden significance*, London, 1968.

back to the *Old Testament* we note there were twelve legitimate rulers called *Judges*. The number twelve is prominent in the description of Solomon's temple, whilst in the *Apocalypse* the heavenly Jerusalem has twelve gates and twelve pearls, whilst the number twelve figures in its sacred dimensions.

In the *Old Testament* it is mentioned that five priests and seven kings were specially anointed. In the *New Testament* Jesus first appears in public at the age of twelve. His appearances after his crucifixion were twelve in number, according to some methods of reckoning.

The followers of the Shiah faith, which flourishes in Persia, and which differ in many ways from other Moslems such as the Sunnis of Arabia and elsewhere, maintain that the Prophet had just twelve successors, whom they call *imams*.[7] The first was Ali, who was reckoned fourth caliph by the Sunnis. He was the son-in-law of Mohammed and is supposed to have had access to secret tradition. He was followed by his sons Hasan and Hasain. All three were martyred. The twelfth imam, Mohammed ibn Hanifiyya went into concealment in A.D. 869 and is expected to reappear in the future. The Imam of the Shiah religion has been compared with the Pope. Both possess infallibility in respect to doctrine, but the Imam was believed to possess the divine gift of impeccability (sinlessness) which the popes certainly have never claimed to possess!

## Poetic Ideas

Whilst some allusions to the number twelve are undoubtedly inspired by occult knowledge, others may be due to more purely mundane requirements. For instance, the alchemists sometimes spoke of the twelve processes of alchemy. As the latter science used many astrological ideas, *e.g.* the metals were called by the names of the planets, it is not surprising that the twelve processes were supposed to be ruled by the twelve

[7] The word imam is used in several different senses, *e.g.* any religious leader or a leader of prayer in a mosque.

signs individually. On the other hand, the division of the year into twelve months, whilst originally based on the zodiac, no longer corresponds therewith in Europe, and is, in any case, only a convenient way of dividing time.

There remain traces of the arcane tradition in many poetical themes, such as the twelve labours of Hercules, the twelve Knights of King Arthur, the twelve paladins of the Emperor Charlemagne, the twelve companions of Odysseus, the twelve shepherds of Romulus, the twelve berserks of Hrolf, etc.

## Scientific Ideas

The number twelve seems to be latent in nature, as revealed in both the physical and the psychological sciences. There are, for instance, many musical scales, but two have become favoured in Western music, the *diatonic* scale of seven, already mentioned as corresponding with the planets, and the *chromatic scale* of twelve, corresponding with the signs of the zodiac, with five additional notes added. Thus the series reads *c*, *c* sharp, d, *e* flat, *e*, *f*, *f* sharp, *g*, *a* flat, *a*, *b* flat, *b*. Similarly there are recognized several additional colours to the sevenfold colour scale already mentioned, and these colours have common names, as being easily recognizable. In fact they come in the same relative positions as in the scale of sounds, so the series reads: crimson, scarlet, orange, yellow, lime, green, turquoise, blue, indigo, violet, purple, magenta.

The present author has also attempted to show that there is some scientific justification for the mediaeval diagrams of the human body marked with the signs of the zodiac and called the *melothesia*.[8] The sequence was Aries the head, Taurus the neck with larynx, Gemini the arms and lungs, Cancer the breasts and stomach, Leo the back and heart, Virgo the belly and intestines, Libra the loins with kidneys, Scorpio the external and internal genitals, Sagittarius, the

[8] The Human Body as a Solar System in *Mysteries of the Ancients,* 18, London, 1945.

hips, thighs with the liver, Capricorn the knees with bones, Aquarius the ankles with the skin and Pisces the feet with the lymphatics.

In another work the author has attempted to show the zodiacal correspondences with the complexes and archetypes of depth psychology,[9] as follows:

Scorpio is represented by the *Manfred complex* of Freud's psycho-analysis and *the shadow* among Jung's archetypes.

Sagittarius is represented by *the Kandaules complex* or motive and the archetype of *the wise old man.*

Capricorn is the *Pan complex* (or *Jehovah complex*) and the archetype of the *mandala,* representing wholeness.

Aquarius is the *Belshazzar complex* (the spoiled child) or the *puer aeternus,* the archetype of the eternally youthful one.

Pisces is the *Don Juan complex* or the archetype of *water,* the unconscious itself.

Aries is the *Phaedra complex* (reminding one of Potiphar's wife) and is a Jungian archetype of the *hobgoblin,* causing nightmares.

Taurus refers to the *Medea complex* and the archetype of *the dwarfs.*

Gemini is connected with the *Clytemnestra complex,* and all opposite polarities including the archetype of *the father and mother.*

Cancer is the *Narcissus complex* and the archetype of *the water-nymph.*

Leo is the *Hercules complex* and the archetype of *the sun-hero.*

Virgo corresponds with the *Amphitryon complex* or St. George and the dragon, and fits in with the archetype of the *virgin* or *treasure.*

Libra in its adverse aspect represents the *Electra complex,* in its more favourable aspect it appears as the archetype of *Paradise.*

[9] The Exploration of the Psyche, *The Astrological Magazine,* Bangalore, India, Jan. 1968.

a.